BLUE HEAVEN

BLUEHEAVEN

ENCOUNTERS WITH THE BLUE POPPY

BILL TERRY

VICTORIA | VANCOUVER | CALGARY

TouchWood
Editions

TouchWood Editions

108 – 17665 66A Avenue	PO Box 468
Surrey, BC V3S 2A7	Custer, WA
www.touchwoodeditions.com	98240-0468

LIBRARY AND ARCHIVES CANADA CATALOGUING IN PUBLICATION

Terry, Bill, 1935–
Blue heaven : encounters with the blue poppy / Bill Terry.
Includes bibliographical references and index. ISBN 978-1-894898-82-9
1. Meconopsis. 2. Terry, Bill, 1935-. I. Title.
QK495.P22T47 2009   635.9'3335   C2008-907720-2

LIBRARY OF CONGRESS CONTROL NUMBER: 2009920167

Edited by Marlyn Horsdal
Proofread by Meaghan Craven
Book design by Jacqui Thomas
Cover and interior photography by Bill Terry

Printed in Canada

TouchWood Editions acknowledges the financial support for its publishing program from
the Government of Canada through the Book Publishing Industry Development Program
(BPIDP), Canada Council for the Arts, and the province of British Columbia through the
British Columbia Arts Council and the Book Publishing Tax Credit.

BRITISH COLUMBIA
ARTS COUNCIL
Supported by the Province of British Columbia

The Canada Council | Le Conseil des Arts
for the Arts | du Canada

"It is a half revealed truth that gardeners,

for the most part, differ from many of their

fellow men in that when success has at

length crowned their efforts, whatever may

have gone before, toil, trial and error,

disappointment after disappointment, failures,

are all swept completely from memory—

obliterated in the ecstasy of pure joy at the

sight of the plants yielding up their

loveliest rewards."

ELSIE REFORD, 1944 [1]

CHAPTER ONE

"THAT LOVELY POPPYWORT"

Of all the deadly occupations
[botanical exploration] is surely the most fatal.

GARDENERS' CHRONICLE, 1881[1]

IN THE LATE SPRING OF 1922, a British Himalayan expedition, working its way along the East Rongbuk Valley in Tibet, encountered big Blue Poppies growing on stony ground at 16,000 feet (4,900 metres). This was not an expedition of plant hunters but a mountaineering team returning from a failed attempt to reach the summit of then-unconquered Mount Everest. A disastrously failed attempt, with the loss of seven Sherpas who were swept to their deaths in an avalanche.

The expedition leader was the legendary mountaineer George Leigh Mallory who, in a letter to his wife, declared himself "half the time in ecstasy" with all that he saw on the descent through the high alpine meadows: "the clear bubbling streams ... things growing as though they liked growing."[2] A lover of nature, he would have been entranced with this encounter with the Blue Poppy.

Strictly speaking, the poppy that Mallory and his party found was not a poppy. It was a meconopsis, a name derived from the Greek *mekon* (poppy) and *opsis* (like). Poppylike. The climbers had found *Meconopsis grandis,* commonly known as the Tibetan Poppy or the Himalayan Blue Poppy.

Mecononopsis grandis: the Himalayan Blue Poppy.

On June 8, 1924, George Leigh Mallory, with his climbing partner Sandy Irvine, vanished into the mists surrounding the summit of Everest, a tragedy that placed him among the pantheon of England's greatest heroes whose triumphs were crowned with death: Admiral Horatio Nelson, Major-General James Wolfe, Robert Falcon Scott. Whether or not Mallory and Irvine reached the top is the most enduring mystery in the annals of mountaineering.

Three-quarters of a century later, on May 1, 1999, Mallory's freeze-dried remains, still clad in tweeds and home-spuns, his leg horribly broken, were found 2,000 feet (six hundred metres) from the peak he may or may not have reached. I like to imagine that pressed in his pocket book were the petals of a big Blue Poppy. •

RIGHT The flowers flutter out like blue-and-gold butterflies.

M. grandis was not entirely unknown in Britain. Seed collected in the Himalayas had been brought to flower at the Royal Botanic Garden, Edinburgh, in 1895. Even so, a quarter of a century later, mastery of its cultivation was still confined to a handful of specialists. Word of the plant may have reached Mallory, but it's unlikely that he or others in his party had ever seen one before.

While Mallory was scaling the battlements of Everest, Frank Kingdon-Ward was battling weather, blood-sucking ticks, biting flies and unruly natives in Burma, Assam and Tibet. Kingdon-Ward (1885–1958) was a professional plant collector and botanist, no less an adventurer than Mallory, no less a brave man capable of great feats of derring-do, but interested in the high alpine meadows more for the plants they yielded than as a route to the world's highest peaks. He was also a very fine writer, recording his explorations and observations with effusive enthusiasm. Some of his books are available in reprint and may be enjoyed by any lover of plants and their origins, while allowance needs to be made for attitudes that befitted an English gentleman of the Empire but today would be denounced by many as, well, politically incorrect.

In the spring of 1924, Kingdon-Ward set out to explore the gorges of the Tsangpo River in southeastern Tibet, the river that, pouring into India, becomes the Brahmaputra. His quest was a legendary waterfall, embedded in Tibetan folklore but never seen by an outsider. The obstacles were formidable: "Every day the scene grew more savage, the mountains higher and steeper."[3] He charted a number of cascades but turned back, defeated by the precipitous roaring gorge, less than a kilometre from where the great falls were eventually discovered. However, the expedition was far from a failure, for among the extensive range of plants he found and subsequently collected was the second species of Himalayan Blue Poppy, *Meconopsis betonicifolia*, which Kingdon-Ward described with typical bravura in his book, *The Riddle of the Tsangpo Gorges*: "Beautiful as were the meadows of the *rong* [valley], a patchwork of colour exhaling fragrance, nevertheless the finest flowers hid themselves modestly under the bushes, along the banks of the stream."[4]

At first he thought the flash of blue was the plumage of a bird. Closer inspection revealed "that lovely poppywort *Meconopsis baileyi* [as it was then named], the woodland blue poppy."[5] Kingdon-Ward, evidently seeing this species for the first time, expressed his delight with breathtaking lyricism: "The flowers flutter out from amongst the sea-green leaves like blue-and-gold butterflies; each is borne singly on a pedicel, the plant carrying half a dozen nodding, incredibly blue-petalled flowers, with a wad of golden anthers in the centre."[6]

One of the qualities that distinguished Kingdon-Ward from other collectors of his day was his knack for spotting a really fine garden plant: "Never have I seen a blue poppy which held out such high hopes of being hardy, and of easy cultivation in Britain … coming from a moderate elevation, it is accustomed to that featureless average of weather which we know so well how to provide it with;"—although many of today's gardeners would consider his expectations over-optimistic—"and being perennial, it will not exasperate gardeners. If it comes easily from self-sown seed, as few species do, it will be perfect."[7]

As Kingdon-Ward wrote that, perhaps there danced in his mind an image of newly leafed-out English woodlands, illuminated with drifts of the naturalized Blue Poppy, mingled with bluebells: a late-spring display to follow the yellow Easter parade of naturalized daffodils and native primroses. But it was not to be. The Blue Poppy showed little inclination to self-seed, proved to be tricky to grow and, though perennial, was often short-lived. He was right about the weather, though—that "featureless average" of Britain's bland climate. The Blue Poppy hates extremes and will expire if it is too hot, too cold, too wet or too dry.

Frank Kingdon-Ward is famous for introducing the Himalayan Blue Poppy to garden cultivation. However, credit for its discovery belongs to the French Jesuit missionary and plant collector Père Jean Marie Delavay, who, in 1886, found Blue Poppies in the alpine woodlands of northwest Yunnan Province, China, and sent pressed specimens to the Museum of Natural History in Paris, where the director, the botanist Adrien René Franchet, named it *Meconopsis betonicifolia* (betony-leaved).

Over fourteen years Franchet received a staggering 200,000 plant specimens from Père Delavay, covering over 4,000 species, of which some 1,500 were new to science. Nor was quality compromised. Franchet declared

Incredibly blue-petalled flowers, with a wad of golden anthers in the centre.

the pressed herbarium specimens to be the best he had received from the field. Moreover, the accompanying descriptive notes were clear and detailed. A pity, then, that Delavay's diligence and thoroughness were not matched by the botanical staff at the museum in Paris. Many shipments remained unopened and unexamined forty years after the priest's death.

Père Delavay's achievement is all the more remarkable considering that he devoted his time first to his duties with Missions Etrangères. Plant collecting was a hobby. He was fortunate, therefore, to be stationed in one of the richest, hitherto botanically unexplored areas of northwest Yunnan. He tramped the surrounding hills over and over, examining every nook and cranny. He travelled alone, carrying a rucksack with little more than a change of socks. Frank Kingdon-Ward, on the other hand, typically "... took stores for six months, these comprising jam, milk, butter, tea, coffee, biscuits, sardines, Quaker oats, potted meat, and chocolate; ... Also a case of rum. Besides these, I took four months' rations, consisting of rice, flour, and ghyi (clarified butter used for cooking); the whole weighing about 1,000 lbs."[8]

Kingdon-Ward was travelling among people who were never far from starvation, so living off the land was not possible, though along the way he was usually able to buy eggs, yak or goat's milk, butter and the occasional tough fowl. So four months' supply had to be carried, a task that required the assistance of the local headman in hiring porters: "... over fifty coolies were required to carry the loads, which included besides the above, tents, bedding, clothes, books, camp furniture, photographic apparatus, oil for lamps, ... botanical presses and quantities of thick paper. My servants comprised a Burmese cook—rather a scallywag—a Kachin 'boy', and a Nung child of fifteen."[9]

Kingdon-Ward was not, however, a wealthy man. He financed his expeditions with sponsorships from nurserymen, such as A. K. Bulley, owner of Bees, the seed company that subsequently made available many of the new, garden-worthy, hardy plants collected by the explorer. Kingdon-Ward sold shares in seed he collected

The London debut of Frank Kingdon-Ward's Blue Poppies was the talk of the town.

WHEN IS A POPPY NOT A POPPY?

The California Poppy is not a poppy. It is *Eschscholzia californica*, named for Johann Friedrich Eschscholz (1793–1831) a physician and naturalist who accompanied Otto von Kotzebue on an around-the-world expedition. Eschscholzia, with six consonants in a row, is a spelling-bee stumper.

The California Tree Poppy is not a poppy. It is *Romneya coulteri*, named in honour of the eighteenth-century Irish astronomer and inventor, the Reverend T. Romney Robinson who served as director of the Armagh Observatory for a remarkable fifty-nine years. A small lunar crater is also named for this good man, assuring him a permanent place in heaven.

The plume poppy is not a poppy. It is *Macleaya cordata*, saluting Alexander Macleay (1767–1848) for twenty-seven years secretary of the Linnean Society in London, then colonial secretary for New South Wales and a lifelong collector of bugs.

The Welsh Poppy is not a poppy. It is a meconopsis: *M. cambrica*, the only European member of a genus of some fifty species, that otherwise all inhabit the high alpine meadows of the Himalayas and mountains to the east—all the way to central China.

All these, however, are included in the poppy family (*Papaveraceae*), along with the true poppies (*Papaver*). A papaver seed pod flips its lid. Meconopsis splits its sides. •

and recruited companions of considerable means, who were ready to foot the bill in exchange for exotic adventure. His companion on the 1924 Tsangpo Gorges expedition was a twenty-four-year-old Scottish aristocrat, John Duncan Vaughan Campbell, fifth Earl of Cawdor, fifteen years Kingdon-Ward's junior and ready for rather more action than plant collecting provided. Cawdor noted in his journal: "It drives me clean daft to walk behind him—stopping every ten yards and hardly moving in between. ... If ever I travel again, I'll make damned sure it's not with a botanist. They are always stopping to gape at weeds."[10]

Cawdor also griped about the food, even though the expedition was in part provisioned by Fortnum & Mason of Piccadilly, purveyors of fine foods to British royalty since the reign of Queen Anne. (Queen Victoria is said to have been especially fond of their take-out meals.) But Lord Cawdor longed for a taste of home cooking: "By God I could do justice to a damned good slab of figgy duff tonight."[11]

In the fall of 1924, the two men and their retinue returned to the site on the banks of the Tsangpo River where Kingdon-Ward had found "that lovely poppy-wort" and harvested the seed. This arrived in England in February 1925, sufficient to be distributed for trial to some fifty expert gardeners throughout Britain. The seed germinated well, and in 1926 the broad, incredibly blue petals unfurled to enraptured applause at the Royal Horticultural Society's spring show. Among the public, there was near pandemonium. Blue Poppy mania had taken root.

The following spring, 1927, enthusiasts were snapping up seedlings of *Meconopsis betonicifolia* at the RHS Chelsea Flower Show for a guinea apiece—a sum equivalent to more than fifty dollars in today's currency. Of course, mature plants were also on display, their ineffable allure quickening the lust of those picturing the poppy as a trophy plant flourishing in their own gardens—or at least those with pockets deep enough to take a flutter on a tiny seedling in a small clay pot. We may reasonably assume that most of those gamblers lost.

Look at it this way: had the Blue Poppy turned out to be the perfect plant Kingdon-Ward hoped for—easy to grow, obligingly long-lived, readily self-seeding —it would have become just another commonplace garden poppy, as familiar as the opium poppy (*Papaver somniferum*) or the Oriental poppy (*Papaver orientalis*). Definitely fetching, but unremarkable.

This image has been digitally
enhanced to depict the dream-like
illusion of the mythical blue flower,
as described by the poet Novalis.

CHAPTER TWO

THE MYTH

The woman who grew Meconopsis
Was asked to give a synopsis.
How can I she cried,
When all of them died,
Do more than perform their autopsies?

MARTHA HOUGHTON, APRIL 1934[1]

THE GERMAN ROMANTIC POET NOVALIS (Fritz von Hardenberg, 1772–1801) prefigured the discovery of the Blue Poppy in his unfinished novel *Heinrich von Ofterdingen*:

> Deep, sweet sleep overpowered him. When he woke he was lying on the soft floor of a valley at the edge of a well. At a little distance, hazy blue cliffs rose with gleaming veins of gold shining through their sides. All around him was a soft mellow light, and the sky above was blue and cloudless. What most attracted him was a lovely blue flower growing at the edge of the well. Its large glossy green leaves overshadowed him. The air was perfumed by the fragrance of flowers of every colour, but he cared for none of them but the blue flower, at which he gazed in tender adoration. As he stood to examine it more closely, it seemed to move and change, the glossy leaves bent down at the stalk and the blossom lent towards him, the petals slowly opened and he saw a lovely, tender face. Amazed at this sight, he

was about to speak when he was aroused by his mother's voice, and he found himself in his own room, the golden light of early day streaming through the casement.[2]

The blue flower, the mythical central image of the poet's dreamlike yearning, was to become the symbol of longing among the Romantics. The blue flower is unattainable.

Just so; the Blue Poppy is the symbol of longing among gardeners and, as we shall see, is widely thought to be unattainable.

"Success with Meconopsis is the crowning achievement of any gardener," declared Graham Stuart Thomas in the US gardening magazine *Horticulture*.[3] Thomas, renowned plantsman, botanical illustrator and author, died in 2003, aged ninety-four, proving once again that great gardeners live to great age.

The image of the Blue Poppy appears in many everyday forms. It adorns chinaware and tableware, tea towels, paper napkins, tiles and clothing. It has twice been depicted on a Canadian stamp. It's a favourite of stained-glass artists. Publishers of garden books that make only passing reference to the Blue Poppy will often select this ineluctably photogenic flower as a cover to seduce the browsing book buyer.

And yet, I cannot think of a plant that's more distinguished by its absence. Most gardeners speak of the Blue Poppy with a sigh, in the past tense, or in the future with a wary sense of hope. Never the present. Just as the Queen pronounced in *Alice Through the Looking Glass*: "The rule is, jam tomorrow and jam yesterday —but never jam today."[4]

The Himalayan Blue Poppy is vanishingly scarce in gardens, even in areas where the climate is suitable. There's no shortage of seed: a single plant can produce hundreds. But ever since 1926, and the excitement that attended the

Meconopsis 'Lingholm', emerging like a butterfly from its cocoon.

exhibition of plants grown from the seed Frank Kingdon-Ward collected in the Tsangpo Gorges of Tibet, the myth has persisted that growing the Blue Poppy is light years beyond the capability of ordinary green fingers. It's up there with squaring the circle and turning lead into gold. Magical arts, special potions, witchcraft have to be conjured. Indeed, had the Blue Poppy been known in the Middle Ages, people might have been burned at the stake for its possession, and the plants thrown on the pyre for good measure.

Graham Stuart Thomas is not alone in perpetuating the myth. In his classic *The Education of a Gardener*, Russell Page tells the story of Thomas Hay, superintendent of the Royal Parks in London, who, in the heady days of Blue Poppy mania, bedded out massed displays in Hyde Park and "... delighted the public with drifts of *Meconopsis betonicifolia*, the blue poppy which ever since his day has been as ardently worked for and is, in town at least, as difficult to succeed with as the philosopher's stone."[5]

And Eleanor Perenyi, biographer of Franz Liszt, in her wonderful collection of essays on gardening, *Green Thoughts*, reserves the category "total disaster ... for the fabled Himalayan poppy. The color of a summer day, with golden anthers—and my abominable snowman. ... I have never seen it—not the tiniest shoot having come up from repeated sowings. ... I would give anything for a glimpse of it, even in somebody else's garden."[6]

I first set eyes on the Blue Poppy in 1968, at Butchart Gardens, near Victoria, BC. This world-famous sunken garden was founded in a worked-out quarry early in the twentieth century by Jenny Butchart, wife of cement manufacturer Robert Pim Butchart, whose appetite for limestone had created the immense crater. There—beyond the clamorous display of Frisbee-sized begonias, beyond the towering delphiniums and stiletto-spurred columbines, beyond the clashing ranks of seven hundred kinds of bedding plant—was a quiet woodland garden. And there stood a drift of the Himalayan Blue Poppy. *Exultate!*

While true poppies can be shattered,
the Blue Poppy casually sloughs off rain.

I had to have this plant in my West Vancouver garden and at once bought a packet of seeds in the Butchart Gardens shop. The next day, carefully following instructions, I started them with great expectations. And watched. And waited. And nothing. Nothing but hopes in tatters. My first attempt to grow the Blue Poppy was a bust.

The Himalayan Blue Poppy is at the top of every plant lover's list: "the dream of every gardener," as Vita Sackville-West put it.[7]

"I'd give anything to grow the Blue Poppy, but I just can't. I bought a package of seed and nothing came up." I hear variations on this sad refrain over and over.

"Where did you get the seed?" I ask. "Oh, from some garden centre or catalogue. I can't exactly remember."

Well, take heart. Often, the fault lies not with the gardener. It lies with commercial seed companies, together with retailers who do not clear off old stock. *They sell dead seed.*

Blue Poppy seed ripens and is ready for harvest in July or August. Allowing time for collection, preparation, packaging and distribution, this fresh seed is unlikely to be on the seller's display rack before November at the earliest. From that point on, the seed, displayed in the warm comfort of the retail outlet, is rapidly losing viability. In fact, unless it is kept cool from the start, by the following March the seed will very likely germinate poorly, or not at all.

Accordingly, Blue Poppy seed bought from a retailer or catalogue between November and February *should* be alive (if not held over from two summers earlier) and *might* germinate if put in the refrigerator and started soon. However, Blue Poppy seed bought between March and October will probably be from the previous year's harvest and likely will be dead on arrival, unless it was kept in cold storage. Just as I did, gardeners buy the packet with the oh-so-seductive cover illustration, start the seed with great expectations and blame themselves when nothing happens.

It was thirty years before I tried again. And then I found out that, given fresh seed, a little learning and a little practice, success with meconopsis is an achievement within the reach of any resolute gardener favoured with suitable climate and soil conditions. True, it's not easy—but the impossibility of growing the Blue Poppy is a myth.

There's not much point in
growing just one or two.

Unlike most Blue Poppies,
'Mrs. Jebb' holds her head high.

CHAPTER THREE

IN THE STEPS OF CHINESE WILSON

*Mountains are the beginning
and end of all natural scenery.*

JOHN RUSKIN[1]

GEORGE MALLORY, WHEN HE ENCOUNTERED the Blue Poppy, stood roughly at the fulcrum of the great mountain rampart that rises as the Hindu Kush in the west, spans Afghanistan, Pakistan's northwest Frontier Province and disputed Kashmir, towers over Nepal, Bhutan and Tibet, and strides on eastward to central China. This range is the home of the Asiatic poppies. At its eastern extremity, the Qionglai Mountains spill from 20,000 feet (6,100 metres) into the fertile plain of the Sichuan Basin.

Here, in May 2000, my wife Rosemary and I joined a small party of fellow members of the Royal Horticultural Society for a "plant-hunting" expedition into the hills of Sichuan that would follow the route taken about one hundred years before by the English plant hunter, Ernest Henry Wilson, nicknamed "Chinese" Wilson. Our leader was a well-known plantsman, John Simmons, O.B.E., for twenty-three years curator of Kew Gardens.

Our party of nine flew to Chengdu, capital of Sichuan, where we were enthusiastically welcomed by our Chinese hosts and expert guides, Professors Yin Kaipu and Zhong Shengxian, from the Chengdu Institute of Biology at the Chinese Academy of Sciences. Dr. Yin, a botanist, spoke no English. Dr. Zhong, a

CHINESE WILSON

Ernest Henry Wilson was working at Kew Gardens in 1898 when his boss, the director, Sir William Thistleton-Dyer, was asked by James Veitch & Sons of Chelsea to recommend an enterprising young man to travel to China. The mission was to collect seeds and cuttings of the legendary handkerchief tree, or dove tree (*Davidia involucrata*), discovered in 1869 by the French missionary and plant explorer Père Jean Pierre Armand David, for whom the tree is named.

As Wilson prepared to set sail in April 1899, the senior Veitch is said to have growled: "My boy, stick to the one thing you are after and do not spend time and money wandering about. Probably almost every worthwhile plant in China has now been introduced into Europe."[2] So Wilson, acting on this instruction, travelled upriver for ten days to the site of the reported davidia, only to find that the rarity he had journeyed halfway round the world to see had been felled. In its place stood a new hut, still faintly redolent of the timber of the dove tree that had been used to build it. Undaunted by this turn of events, Wilson persisted in the quest and a month later found a cliff-side grove of dove trees—and additionally, in the course of this expedition, some four hundred new plant species.

In this, and later expeditions, Chinese Wilson introduced over 1,500 plants to cultivation, including many of today's standard garden plants. His methods were certainly thorough. For example, in his fourth expedition in 1910, collecting the ethereally fragrant, white regal lily (*Lilium regale*), Wilson marked 6,000 plants along the banks of the Min River and returned after the foliage had died down to dig up all 6,000 bulbs for dispatch to his delighted American employer. Today we regard such plunder with disfavour. However, the lily still survives in this area as we saw in May 2000, albeit on cliff-hanging ledges that only a goat could reach. •

biologist, was our interpreter. A celebratory banquet was held in our honour. There were speeches, toasts, gifts exchanged, more speeches. Next morning we drove into the mountains. A century ago, Wilson followed faint trails on horse-back, with a retinue of guides, bearers, mules and oxen, carrying the customary impedimenta of the European plant hunters: tents, camp bed and bedding, food, clothing, books and botanical equipment, including the heavy and fragile glass "Wardian cases" or terrariums, used by collectors to keep plants alive during the long voyage home. We followed potholed roads in a Toyota mini-bus, with sealed plastic bags of junk snacks that popped as we gained altitude.

In the foothills we visited the Panda Research Station at Wolong. An American crew was at work, filming for *National Geographic* and, of necessity, faking natural habitat. The panda, although the world's most loved, cuddly creature, is nonetheless gravely threatened with extinction in the wild. Dr. Yin told us that in thirty years of plant hunting in the mountains he had only once seen the animal. Its population was estimated then to be a mere 1,500, its survival acutely endan-gered by habitat loss and poaching. Dr. Zhong said that in China, conviction of killing a panda can carry the death penalty. People occasionally bring one, injured or sick and starving, to Wolong for expert care and rehabilitation. The research station also runs a successful breeding program, but, as we were told, there's a frustrating lack of success with reintroducing the animals to the wild.

From Wolong we drove up, up and up, twisting back and forth, thirty miles (fifty kilometres) on a narrow, handmade, concrete road, looping like flung spaghetti, to the Ba Lang Shan Pass at 14,500 feet (4,400 metres). As we climbed, we stopped here and there to "botanize," finding primulas and arisaemas and a blue corydalis that looked like the cultivar 'Blue Panda' and had its beeswax fragrance, too. John Simmons explained that China had been closed to Western plant hunters since the 1930s, and we were quite likely to find unclassified species. I was impatient to get above the tree line. There, above 10,000 feet (3,000 metres), we were likely to see Asiatic poppies in bloom, though not the perennial blue species, which are only to be found far to the west. Wilson had collected the yellow Lampshade Poppy (*Meconopsis integrifolia*) in this region.

The world's most loved, cuddly
creature: a panda at Wolong.

A final stand of Chinese larch and over the next ridge the meadows lay before us: an open, treeless landscape of rocky scree and grass, closely cropped by yaks that were grazing nearby. And scattered like yellow Smarties to the horizon, the Lampshade Poppy in full flower. Luckily, these were not on the yak menu. On this side of the pass, at about 12,000 feet (3,700 metres), these poppies were only a foot high, yet crowned with a bright, butter-yellow flower, fully six inches (fifteen centimetres) across. The huge flower, usually just one, stood on a leafless stalk rising from a rosette of hairy, yellow-green leaves.

This version of *M. integrifolia* was very different from the typical bulky, multi-flowered form that we found beyond the Ba Lang Shan Pass. There, some 2,000 feet (six hundred metres) lower, the plant stood thirty inches (seventy-five centimetres) tall, with a very stout main stem erupting from the basal rosette, then branching at the top into several leafless stalks, each bearing a cupped, yellow flower.

A few days later, still above 10,000 feet (3,000 metres), we were dodging potholes and bouncing in low gear along a barely navigable dirt road, west

The Panda Research Station at Wolong is a mere six miles (ten kilometres) from the epicentre of the 7.9-magnitude earthquake that devastated much of Sichuan Province in May 2008. Terrified tourists described the surrounding cliffs exploding with rock avalanches. "These rocks were just flying through the air. Some were the size of Volkswagens."[3] Miraculously, all the pandas—and the tourists—survived. •

ABOVE, LEFT *M. integrifolia* at 12,000 feet (3,700 metres)—a stunted plant with one huge flower.

OPPOSITE The Lampshade Poppy, beyond the Ba Lang Shan Pass.

The Red Poppywort that
meconopsis fanciers rave about.

of Songpan. (Of all the places we stayed in, Songpan alone we remember with disgust, due to the grubby condition of the town and, particularly, the crucified pelts of the rare and protected snow leopard displayed outside souvenir shops for the delectation of Chinese tourists. Dr. Zhong was furious: "If I were the Governor of Sichuan, I'd have the Mayor of Songpan on the carpet.") Our route, taking us deeper into the mountains, followed a long, green valley. A limpid stream threaded quietly back and forth, twisting through the alpine pasture. Clear blue sky, open country, no trees, few shrubs. Occasional groups of grazing yak. Not too promising for plant hunting—till we noticed splashes of brilliant red here and there, as if weekend warriors had been firing paint balls at the grass. We shouted for a halt, grabbed cameras and tumbled out of the vehicle, for this was the Asiatic poppy that meconopsis fanciers rave about: *M. punicea*, occasionally called the Red Poppywort. Just a few, scattered plants had luckily escaped the trampling hooves.

The flower of this delicate poppy defines the colour red. It has just four elliptical petals that look as if they need ironing. They fall like silk flags on

Among plants, none display such a palette of pure primary colours as the Asiatic poppies. There is no red redder than the red of *punicea*, no yellow more buttery than *integrifolia*. The white of *superba* is whiter than white. The imperial purples of *lancifolia* and *delavayi* are unmatched. No blue can compare with the blue of a perfect *grandis* or *betonicifolia*.

The size of the flowers is also exceptional. George Taylor, who, in 1934, published the first comprehensive account of meconopsis, offers an explanation: "It is a general feature of alpine plants that they produce comparatively large, brilliantly coloured flowers, and the species of *Meconopsis* are no exception. The more extensive exposure to light has been suggested as a reason, but it may also be partly accounted for as a device to increase the chances of insect visitation, which must be at a premium under the extreme conditions existing at high altitudes."[4] •

a windless day, or a butterfly's wings hung out to dry. The flower trembles atop a stalk that looks too thin to bear its weight. It is, as we shall see, a formidable challenge for the Pacific Northwest coast gardener.

"This adventure has paid for itself if I never see another flower," said an exuberant fellow enthusiast.

But there was more to come just round the corner—another poppy, a purple species none of us could name. Dr. Yin, riffling through the pages of his five-volume encyclopaedia of Chinese flora, pronounced this to be *Meconopsis henrici* (named for the French botanist and explorer, Prince Henri d'Orléans). We had no reason to challenge his identification, for none of us had seen this plant before and we knew that our ghostly guide, Chinese Wilson, had collected seed of *M. henrici* in this valley in 1904. However, Dr. Yin was a shrub and tree expert and, as we eventually realized, hardly more knowledgeable than ourselves on other plant forms. To be fair, Dr. Yin was doing his frantic best to keep up with looking up and naming the profusion of flowers, shoots and leaves we all were heaping upon him, but very often his identification was a hasty guess.

The December 2002 issue of the Royal Horticultural Society's journal, *The Garden*, revealed a different provenance for this poppy. In 1993 Christopher Grey-Wilson, leading a party of plant hunters in western Sichuan came across a poppy which "was first taken to be *M. henrici* which we had seen a few days earlier. ... Closer scrutiny revealed differences, such as the somewhat nodding, more deeply cupped flowers. However, most noticeable was the dark blotch at the back of each petal, giving the centre of the flower a dark maroon-black 'eye'."[5]

After further investigation, and rigorous analysis and debate, it was determined by the international committee that rules on these matters that this was indeed a new species, and in 2002 the name *Meconopsis sinomaculata* (Chinese/spotted) was officially bestowed.

It was a surprise that any species of Asiatic poppy remained to be discovered, some sixty years after the last, and an even bigger surprise that such fine plant collectors as Chinese Wilson and Reginald Farrer (1880–1920), travelling in this same valley, had overlooked it. However, for over half of the twentieth century, throughout the Japanese occupation and Mao's long rule, foreign exploration was banned. Chinese botanists were not encouraged to fill the gap, and discovery and identification of new species from China accordingly slowed to a trickle.

Another surprise came in July 2005, when a party from Britain's Alpine Garden Society, working the foothills to the east of Mount Everest, provided the necessary documentation —photographs and pressed plant parts—to add *Meconopsis tibetica* to the portfolio. Their discovery of this rich, wine-red poppy was really a rediscovery of a species described by the leader of the 1921 British expedition, the first of three unsuccessful assaults from the Tibet side on Everest's implacable north face. Yes, George Leigh Mallory was part of the team, though not its leader. That was Charles Howard-Bury, an Irish explorer and botanist, who encountered a "... wonderful meconopsis of a deep claret colour that I had never seen before. There were fifteen to twenty flowers on each stem and it grew from two to three feet."[6]

Asiatic poppies grow at altitudes of 10,000 feet (3,000 metres) or more, across the breadth of south-central temperate Asia, an area comprising much of China and extending west into

A new discovery—*Meconopsis sinomaculata.*

31

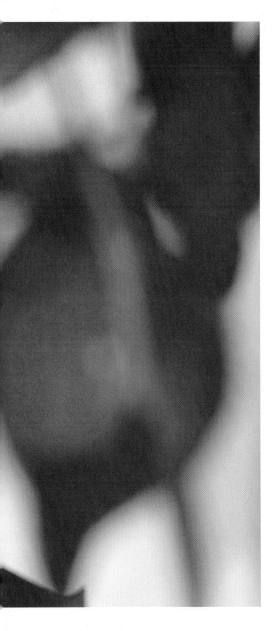

mountainous regions of neighbouring states, such as Bhutan, Nepal and northern Burma. Some species are very wide ranging, while others lay claim to a relatively small territory. It is probable that somewhere in this extraordinarily rich botanical hunting ground, perhaps in a stony meadow or patch of woodland in a remote mountain valley, a meconopsis species, new to science, still awaits collection and identification by some twenty-first-century plant explorer.

M. punicea. On a long, slender stem, the Red Poppywort flutters in a breeze.

CHAPTER FOUR

THE BLUE POPPY

A stream of Blue Poppies,
dazzling as sapphires in the pale light.

FRANK KINGDON-WARD[1]

THE BLUE POPPY COMES IN various forms. In the wild, identification is relatively straightforward. In cultivation, confusion and misidentification abound.

In the wild are found two distinct, large, perennial species, both commonly known as the Himalayan Blue Poppy, or sometimes the Tibetan Poppy. Both are blue and beautiful. Both hail from the Himalayas and mountain meadows, eastward as far as western China. The one that George Leigh Mallory encountered on the second Everest expedition in 1922 is *Meconopsis grandis*. The other, introduced from seed brought by Frank Kingdon-Ward from the Tsangpo River Gorges expedition in 1924, is *M. betonicifolia*.

These two species are somewhat variable, depending on where they are found, especially *M. grandis,* which blooms in many shades of blue and purple and varies in height from about 18 inches to 4 feet (45 to 120 centimetres). In some cultivated

The species *M. betonicifolia* will come
true from seed.

It's easy to tell the seed pods apart.
FROM LEFT TO RIGHT *M. betonicifolia,
M. grandis, M. 'Lingholm'*

According to Sir George Taylor, whose 1934 monograph on the genus *Meconopsis* is still an essential reference, the first specimens of *M. grandis* to arrive in Britain in the 1880s were *cultivated*. They were growing in the Himalayan kingdom of Sikkim at 11,000 feet (3,400 metres), around the huts of shepherds who "are not primarily concerned with the aesthetic qualities of the plant, but grow it rather for the extraction of oil from the seeds, although the properties of this oil are not recorded."[2] •

RIGHT

A lovely white form (*M. betonicifolia* var. *alba*) is an occasional occurrence.

forms, the flowers, up to five inches (thirteen centimetres) across, are borne singly on tall, bare stems, rising from a basal rosette. However, experts believe that the "true *grandis*" bears a whorl of small leaves near the top of the stem, with one to three pendant flowers growing from this junction on short stems. A number of characteristics distinguish *M. grandis* from other big Blue Poppies. The anthers, which make up the golden centre of the flower, are sometimes tightly packed, firm to the touch. The leaves are stiffly upright and covered with fine hairs, lance-shaped, long and narrow, pointed at the top and attached to the stem like ears without lobes. In some, the leaves are shallowly notched along the edges. The seed pods are exceptionally large, oblong and smooth. And here's the most curious and, as far as I know, unique habit of this poppy: after the petals have dropped, the stalk straightens and lengthens, reaching as much as two feet (sixty-one centimetres) higher. Why would such a mutation be selected for survival? Well, the effect may be aesthetically ungainly and unbalanced, but the prospects of reproduction are improved because the ripening seed pod is held clear of the early autumn snows, which blanket

the high Himalayan meadows where this species grows at altitudes from 10,000 to 17,000 feet (3,000 to 5,200 metres).

On the Pacific Northwest coast, *Meconopsis grandis* is the first Blue Poppy to flower, as early as late March. *M. betonicifolia,* by far the more familiar of the two, begins its parade a month later. It's also variable in colour with a lovely white form occasionally occurring. (In our garden, where spontaneous hybridization is entirely likely, I once found a freak with blue petals blurring into white at the edges. I dropped it from the gene pool.) The flowers, typically 3 to 4 inches (7 to 10 centimetres) across, are smaller, much more numerous, more up-facing and less cupped than those of *M. grandis.* The edges of the petals are often frilled. The leaves are hairy, like those of *M. grandis,* but otherwise quite different: broader, with serrated edges, slightly pointed or rounded at the top and usually cordate, heart-shaped where they join the stem. To put it another way, the leaves have earlobes; those of *M. grandis* do not. The seed capsule is hairy and barrel shaped. *M. betonicifolia* is native to northwest Yunnan, where it was first found, as well as neighbouring areas of Tibet and Burma at altitudes from 10,000 to 13,000 feet (3,000 to 4,000 metres).

The two big Blue Poppy species are strangers to the wild. Their ranges do not overlap, as far as we know. But living things are programmed to spread their genes. Introduced to each other in British gardens in the early 1930s, the species took full advantage of their propinquity, proving to be compatible and without inhibition in getting intimately acquainted. The encounter turned out to be no less advantageous to gardeners, for a number of particularly desirable, exceptionally beautiful Blue Poppies have resulted from some seventy generations of random and largely undocumented hybridizing, of crossing and recrossing. As a result, in cultivation today there's a great diversity of hybrids between the two parent species, very likely also flavoured with a pinch of a less distinguished blue-flowered species, *Meconopsis simplicifolia.*

M. betonicifolia consistently breeds true from seed, and plants or seed of this species are usually correctly labelled. *M. grandis,* however, is a promiscuous and inconsistent plant that in cultivation has essentially hybridized itself into near extinction. The name lingers on in nursery catalogues and seed lists, but the labelling will almost certainly be incorrect. The true species is rarely met, except in specialist meconopsis collections where, ideally, the plant is grown far enough away from other Blue Poppies to reduce the chances of cross-pollination, or else raised from pedigree seed known to have been collected in the wild.

George Sherriff and Frank Ludlow, plant explorers who together undertook several collecting expeditions in the mid-twentieth century, found a particularly fine form of *M. grandis* in the Himalayan Kingdom of Bhutan in 1934. Sherriff bagged a few flower seed heads and returned some weeks later to collect the seed, only to find that yaks had eaten the plants, bags and all. So he searched the area and harvested seed from other specimens, which he believed to be similar. This famous collection was given the lot number *M. grandis* GS 600. To this day, you may see seed listed under this name. It is misnamed. Fertile poppies derived from this collection no longer exist.

However, some of the finest *infertile* hybrid Blue Poppies currently in cultivation are believed to be derived from Sherriff's famous seed lot. Being sterile, they can be propagated only by division, hence they are rare and almost entirely confined to the British Isles. The names of the sterile clones

In *Plant Hunting on the Edge of the World*, Frank Kingdon-Ward commented on the differences between wild and cultivated *M. betonicifolia*: "Amongst the hundreds of plants I saw [in the wild], I never saw one with anything but azure blue flowers or with more than four petals. In Britain, on the other hand, there is sometimes a tendency for the flowers to come purple—a ruinous colour."[3] He speculated that this was due to lime in the soil or over-feeding. Kingdon-Ward also observed "a strong tendency toward doubling" in cultivation.

Indeed there is, and it's a regrettable tendency. Doubling is not an attractive feature in the flower because it contradicts the economy of form, the essential simplicity that is one of the plant's most endearing characteristics. The Blue Poppy carries no spare parts. •

in the "George Sherriff Group" include *Meconopsis* 'Jimmy Bayne', 'Huntfield', 'Ascreavie' and 'Barney's Blue'. These hybrids and many other infertile forms of the Blue Poppy have arisen by chance: serendipitous discoveries in the gardens of meconopsis fanciers.

Typical is the story of W. G. Sheldon, an English gardener who lived in Oxted, Surrey. In 1934 he noticed a new and distinctive plant, a cross between the Nepal form of *M. grandis* and *M. betonicifolia*. Indeed, similar hybrids sprang up in several gardens in the mid-1930s, but Sheldon was the first to report it to the Royal Horticultural Society, which verified the originality and stunning quality of the plant and named it for the lucky grower—*Meconopsis* × *sheldonii*. You will find this famous hybrid still touted in plant and seed catalogues. However, as a fertile plant, it is long lost. As with *M. grandis*, seventy years of garden cultivation and undocumented hybridizing have led to its probable extinction. Any offering of *M.* × *sheldonii* may prove to be fertile and may turn out to be blue, but it will not grow into the plant claimed. The seed I started under that name grew into *M. betonicifolia*.

Also bogus are seeds or plants offered under the name *M.* 'Crewdson's Hybrid,' a cross that occurred in Cicely M. Crewdson's Cumbrian garden in 1938, between the Sikkim form of *M. grandis* and *M. betonicifolia*. This plant and its true descendants long ago stopped producing fertile seed and, while the genuine 'Crewdson's Hybrid' Blue Poppy does exist as an *infertile* plant, anything grown from seed today under that name will turn out to be *M. betonicifolia*. Various other invalid names appear from time to time. I've seen 'Heavenly Blue', 'Blue Ice' and 'Patterson's Blue'—names that may have been put into circulation by a nursery looking for a fetching new moniker, or by a gardener attaching his name to seed offered to a seed exchange. And these impostors can be carried into the next generation and passed around like second-hand smoke.

There is a named *fertile* hybrid, and a very fine one too. In the early 1960s, *Meconopsis* 'Lingholm' arose in a Lake District garden, in northern England, due to a chance doubling of chromosomes in an *infertile* hybrid, which resulted in a restoration of fertility. Doubling to 246. It's a wonder this plant doesn't walk and talk.

While *M. grandis* is an important and necessary plant for collectors and

M. grandis is very variable,
blooming in a range of purple
and blue shades.

Meconopsis betonicifolia is sometimes listed as *M. baileyi,* or *M. betonicifolia* var. *baileyi*. This is a holdover from the early twentieth century when it was thought that there were two species rather than, as was eventually determined, one with geographical variations.

Bailey was Major Frederick M. Bailey, a British army officer, political attaché in Sikkim, dauntless explorer and presumed spy, who, in 1913, scrambled forty miles (sixty-four kilometres) into the Tsangpo Gorges in Tibet before turning back, ravaged by fever, leeches and near-starvation. Among his souvenirs was a single Blue Poppy flower, pressed in his pocket book, which he sent to Sir David Prain at Kew. Upon this fragmentary and damaged evidence, as well as the fact that it was collected some three hundred miles (five hundred kilometres) distant from Père Delavay's 1886 discovery, Prain based his conclusion that this was a species distinct from *M. betonicifolia* and accordingly named it *M. baileyi*.

The major met Frank Kingdon-Ward at the start of the latter's Tsangpo Gorges quest with Lord Cawdor in 1924 and shared the stories of his own journey, thirteen years earlier. He told Kingdon-Ward where to find the poppy that bore his name. However, it became clear, after Kingdon-Ward sent home the seed and plant material he had collected in the same region, labelled as he believed it to be, *M. baileyi,* that it and the earlier-named *M. betonicifolia* were geographical variations of the same species.

A Canadian sequel: if stories of the early years of the Butchart Gardens are more truth than fancy, Bailey must also, at some time, have collected and sent home seed of the Blue Poppy that at that time bore his name. The drifts of Himalayan poppies at Butchart Gardens are claimed to be direct descendants of seed sent by Bailey to the Royal Botanic Garden, Edinburgh. It is also reported that in the 1930s, Bailey lunched with the Butcharts and saw his poppies in bloom. No doubt Bailey did lunch with the Butcharts, but I have found no record of him travelling into the land of the Blue Poppies after 1913, and it's more likely that the seeds Jenny Butchart acquired were descendants of the widely distributed Kingdon-Ward collection.

Perhaps in homage to this connection, Butchart Gardens still sell Blue Poppy seed, quaintly, though incorrectly, labelled *Meconopsis baileyi*. •

botanists, in my view it falls short of 'Lingholm' as a highly desirable garden plant. This hybrid is magnificent. It bears several flowers on short stalks, from a whorl of leaves near the top of the stem. Additional buds may appear lower down wherever a leaf joins the stem (the leaf axils). The flowers are typically a deeply saturated sky blue, pendant, cup shaped and large, up to six inches (fifteen centimetres) across, or exceptionally 7.5 inches (twenty centimetres). Shyly, the flowers hang their heads. At its best *M.* 'Lingholm' is a most beautifully proportioned plant. Its manner is demure, polite. The whole—leaves, stem and flower—combines in perfect harmony.

Every plant family has its enthusiasts and those enthusiasts find each other and organize to share expertise and to advance the study and development of their chosen genus. There's the Saxifrage Society and the Cyclamen Society, the Lily Group and the Fritillaria Group. Some, such as the Primula Society, are venerable organizations with records dating back to the nineteenth century. There are several Rhododendron Societies and many, many more such

There's a reason the Asiatic poppies hang their heads.

The flowers of their cousins, the true poppies (*Papaver*), are held brazenly up-facing, taunting the sky to do its worst. They get away with it at home in the Mediterranean region, where many of the garden favourites originate. The Oriental poppies (*Papaver orientalis*), for example, come from Turkey and northern Iran. There they can count on warm, dry weather in blooming time. But in cultivation, to the gardener's despair, one thunder shower and the party's over, leaving only the shattered wreckage of yesterday's glory.

Not so meconopsis. As Frank Kingdon-Ward observed in early July in Tibet: "All the poppies were now flowering together, and though the heavy sky rained ramrods on them, they cared little."[4] July, in fact, is the peak month of the monsoon season—the wettest month of the year, with August in second place. The poppies are well adapted to these conditions and, with bowed heads, slough off the rain most effectively. Nor will the leaves be flattened in pounding rain. Protected by a pelt of fine bristles, they actually remain more or less dry because water, held away by the bristles, gathers in tiny spheres that quickly skitter off like beads of quicksilver. •

The fertile hybrid, *M.* 'Lingholm',
is a superb garden plant.

assemblies. So it's no great surprise to find The Meconopsis Group, at its core a small but vital cabal of the world's leading experts on the Asiatic poppies. It was founded in Scotland in 1998, and among its first aims was sorting out the long-standing confusion and chaos in naming the big blue perennial poppies.

Over several years, in collaboration with the Royal Botanic Garden, Edinburgh (RBGE), the group undertook comprehensive investigation of the Blue Poppies, of both sterile hybrids and seed-raised forms. Members donated plants that were lined out, for comparison, in a trial bed at RBGE. They conducted seed trials and took notes and photographs of plant parts, both above and below ground, at all stages of development.

They compared results, using dried herbarium specimens at the RBGE archives, including plants originally pressed in the field by collectors such as Frank Kingdon-Ward and George Sherriff, today the only means of directly studying the ancestral poppies. They counted chromosomes. And they made progress in sorting out the confusion in identities and naming.

Their preliminary recommendations, published in 2002, were adopted by the Royal Horticultural Society. Properly speaking, names for *fertile* large Blue Poppies are now limited to the species (*MM. grandis* and *betonicifolia*), and the collective description Fertile Blue Group, which describes any seed-raised, fertile hybrid including 'Lingholm'. However, the nursery trade balked. They thought the term Fertile Blue Group would be insufficiently marketable. To the customer, they argued, it would have all the appeal of yesterday's cold porridge. A compromise was reached. All fertile blue hybrids and their seed may be offered as *Meconopsis* 'Lingholm', until further study reveals other distinctive, nameable hybrids.

The hybrid sterile clones are listed in two groups: the George Sherriff Group, comprising those big blue perennial poppies thought to have descended from the GS 600 seed lot and the Infertile Blue Group, which includes the rest of the named sterile clones, such as 'Mrs Jebb', 'Slieve Donard', 'Crewdson's Hybrid' and several others.

So, as this brief tale of seven decades of garden promiscuity and unbridled lust suggests, the Blue Poppy blooms in many subtle variations. For most gardeners, however, any Blue Poppy will do, and some are prepared to take extreme measures to grow it.

ABOVE 'Mrs. Jebb' is a sterile hybrid,
catalogued in the Infertile Blue Group.

OPPOSITE Variations on the theme
of *Meconopsis* 'Lingholm'.

CHAPTER FIVE

DESPERATE MEASURES

To grow the Blue Poppy, I would have to move house, but it is a plant of such dreamlike beauty that I sometimes think it would be worth it.

ANNE SCOTT-JAMES[1]

STROLLING THE BOULEVARDS OF THE Internet, one can drop in on chat rooms, where growers (or would-be growers) of the Himalayan Blue Poppy gather to exchange ideas and seek help. Denys, who gardens in Normandy, reports on his technique for starting seeds: "The method I have followed is to try to reproduce the Himalayan weather. Sow the seeds on special earth. Keep moisture, within around 10°C during two weeks. Then cover them with a thin coat of ice, put them one week into your refrigerator (freezer). This operation will break the seed's skin. Take them out and keep them within 15°C to 18°C, always with moist earth. I hope you'll also get success."

Denys goes on to admit that most of his tiny seedlings died within a few days of appearing. James, another participant, suggests that this is almost certainly caused by damping off, a fungal disease that can infect and speedily kill all seedlings, especially those germinated in overcrowded, poorly ventilated conditions.

The drop-dead blue of 'Mrs. Jebb'.

Nobody comments on Denys's efforts to reproduce the Himalayan conditions, but all this trouble is quite unnecessary. For, while Blue Poppies evolved in the Himalayas, it doesn't follow that emulating their home environment will produce the best results in cultivation. Indeed, there are countless stories of emigrant plants (and creatures) running amok when let loose in other lands, apparently more than happy to go forth and multiply.

Blue Poppies have never become invasive, but when garden-raised and tended in a suitable climate, they're more likely to thrive than wildlings exposed to the vagaries of nature in the alpine meadows of home. Survival there is precarious. That is why they are profligate seed producers, with most of the seed to be scattered and wasted. In the plant's native habitat, at elevations above 10,000 feet (3,000 metres), where in some years snow never entirely melts away, perhaps one in a hundred seeds will

'Mrs. Jebb' and 'Crarae' are both singularly pretty and (being sterile), prettily single.

grow into a mature plant—which is all that's needed to ensure the survival of the species.

Alice is on-line to share her success. She says she bought her first Blue Poppy in May as a plant in bloom and set it out on the east side of her house in a sheltered location. "A nursery employee told me the blue poppies don't like the crown to get wet over the winter and suggested that when the cold and wet weather came to put slug bait around it and cover it with a large clay pot. She said it should be a clay pot so it wouldn't fly away in the wind. I did as she suggested and was rewarded this year with two stalks and several beautiful blooms."

Verity replies that she thinks Alice may be mixing cause and effect. "The plant doubling in size has nothing to do with giving it a clay hat. I agree though, it's unlikely to take flight." Verity adds that she thinks the pot is unnecessary. "I don't believe Blue Poppies mind the crown getting wet, provided the water quickly drains away. What's fatal in winter (indeed fatal at any time of year) is crown rot, the result of standing in a waterlogged bed. Poor drainage. Few plants like wet feet. In the case of meconopsis it's deadly. Prepare the soil well, digging in lots of humus and you won't need the pot."

Karin, from coastal British Columbia, asks the question that always worries gardeners in her region: "Does anybody know how they do around deer? We have a herd of them in our yard. One mom keeps on coming back year after year and always has twins. Sigh. It would be sad to get some and have them munched up by the deer."

Gardeners report that deer will eat anything if they're hungry enough. I don't doubt they would find Blue Poppies mighty toothsome. Meconopsis have not been exploited for human food, but people of the region where they grow, perhaps in times of scarcity, have been known to cook and eat the buds and young shoots of some species. As for deer, they may not kill the plant as they graze the tender, juicy shoots and young leaves, but flowering, at least for that year, will be cancelled.

A burst of gold surrounded by the most unearthly blue.

It can't sing. It can't dance. It can't clown, juggle or ride a unicycle. All it can do it stand there and look blue. Still, in the heart of the US prairie, people *pay* to see it do just that.

CHAMPAIGN, ILL. — Area flower lovers are invited to get a close-up look at one of the world's rare true blue flowers, the Meconopsis, known more widely as the Himalayan Blue Poppy, Saturday and Sunday (March 20–21) at the Plant Biology Conservatory at the University of Illinois at Urbana-Champaign.

"Admission will be three dollars to see the flower known as the 'elusive butterfly of the garden' and find out what makes this poppy so rare that it grows in only a few areas of the world," said Deborah Black, manager of the plant biology greenhouses. The Himalayan Blue Poppy Show will be open from 9 AM to 5 PM both days.

Central Illinois is a region entirely hostile to the cultivation of meconopsis. In the annals of Blue Poppydom, growing it there would stand as a truly amazing achievement. I contacted Debbie Black to learn more.

"I'm one of those people who drool over the blue poppies," she wrote. "Blue is my favourite color and the Blue Poppy is one of those rare, truly blue flowers. I can't grow the poppy here in central Illinois. The climate is all wrong.

"Three years ago the university was hit with huge cuts. My funds were slashed almost 75 per cent. I knew a lot of gardeners out there feel as I do about the Blue Poppy and thought it might make a good fundraiser if I could work out a way of putting on a display. I did a search to find out about growing them. There wasn't a lot out there. Just saying they like cool, moist conditions doesn't help much in Illinois. Since I had no experience, I didn't want to risk a lot of money and then watch all the poppies die."

Debbie bought plants from a nursery in Alaska and over-wintered them in the greenhouse, hoping she could keep the plants alive long enough to bring them to flower.

"I started small, buying 40 plants. Only 24 flowered. Even so, I had a good crowd. Around 180 came out, and they all enjoyed it since you don't see blue poppies in Illinois.

"This year, I ordered 80 poppies. Over 300 came to the show. It was sensational, with 40 plants in bloom; larger and bluer this time. (I used more fertilizer and water. Every year is a chance to learn more.) The response was terrific. People took pictures and you could see the excitement on their faces. Everyone raved and there's no complaint about paying.

"Right now I'm trying to keep the poppies alive through this scorching summer. The first year they all died within three weeks of the show. This year, I'm playing with room conditions and water to see if I can keep any alive. After four months I still have forty plants, though they don't look too perky. Right now, I have them in a cooler at 45°F/7°C. I'm gonna play with these plants, testing different conditions to improve on future shows."

Well, theoretically, with appropriate artificial control of light and temperature, Blue Poppies could be grown anywhere on Earth. Whether or not they *should* be again raises the modern moral dilemma: how much greenhouse gas emission is justified for the pursuit of pure pleasure? •

In another chat room, on another day, are gathered the obsessed, the desperate, the hard-core enthusiasts—such as Glenn, who gardens in Melbourne, Australia, and fell for the poppy on a visit to New Zealand.

"Awesome," he says. "I can't find the words, except I've just got to have it for my garden. Trouble is none of the garden centres here in Melbourne have it and most haven't even heard of it. Nobody seems to have any seed either. Can somebody send me some?"

Beverley suggests Glenn might have to move to southern Tasmania to grow his dream poppy, kindly pointing out that there's a good reason he can't find it in Melbourne: Meconopsis won't grow there. Summers in New South Wales are far too hot and dry, while winters are insufficiently cold.

Bob, joining the discussion from Ontario, *can* find the words. "How do I feel when I run across a true blue? My first sight of a true blue meconopsis simply took my breath away. A burst of gold surrounded by the most unearthly blue. And why do I struggle with meconopsis? Perhaps to relive the thrill of that moment."

A totally unsuitable climate won't stop Paddy, who lives in the northern part of Utah, near the Idaho border—high desert country. "You'll think I'm crazy, and I know they're not supposed to be able to grow here, but I have a plan to create a pocket in my half-acre backyard to plant and nurture these babies. There's a nice stand of trees in the back that I think I could use as the basis to develop a little microclimate. I intend to invest in a misting machine to keep the area cool and moist. And if I need to, I'll look into how to 'refrigerate' or cool the little area in other ways during our hot dry summers. I guess I'm obsessed, but ever since I saw the meconopsis five years ago, I've been dying to cultivate them."

Beverley again, while pointing out that such drastic measures may be rather costly to the planet in carbon emissions, agrees it may be worth a try. She notes that the Pacific Northwest coast, particularly Alaska, is the best region in the United States for cultivating Blue Poppies.

M. betonicifolia 'Hensol Violet' is a fertile variation named for Hensol Castle in Scotland, where it first appeared.

Meconopsis may be cultivated in a climate such as that prevailing along the Pacific Northwest coast from Washington State to Alaska, or with particular success in northern Scandinavia or Scotland, where a summer temperature above 20°C is the occasion for three days of national rejoicing. They are seen here and there in coastal New England and may be grown in Ulster and Iceland. They will do well in the northern counties of England, or southern New Zealand. They may be happy in northern Japan and in pockets of Patagonia. These parts of the world share cool summer days and cooler nights.

A cool, moist summer best replicates the season of mist and monsoon rains that bathes the Himalayan Blue Poppies during the growing months in their alpine meadows, while in winter the dormant buds and rosettes rest cosily beneath a blanket of several feet of snow.

Some nursery catalogues—a genre much given to embellishment—list Blue Poppies as hardy to Zone 3, regions where winter temperatures may plunge to -40°C. In North America that includes a broad swath of the Prairies, where, under a scant covering of blowing snow, the ground may freeze to a metre's depth. In the improbable event the poppies survive this treatment, they may be finished off in the thaw, when melting snow pools on the impervious, still-frozen surface. Equally fatal are the scorching days and hot nights of summer. It just may be possible that some hopelessly enraptured slave of the Blue Poppy—such as Paddy of Utah—could, by providing winter shelter and constant summer misting, nurse an exhausted and stunted plant or two into bloom under these conditions. But I have not heard of such triumphs.

In regions of deeper snow and somewhat milder winters, some success in growing Blue Poppies can be won by a skilled and persistent gardener. I've read of such achievements in both Edmonton and Calgary. Down east, the Blue Poppy is cultivated here and there in New England, while Gerald Taaffe of Ottawa writes: "The secret for me has been, firstly, to start the seeds early and keep them growing strongly, so that I have nice, fat, fuzzy plants to put out in mid-June. Then too, it helps to work coarse, acid sand and compost into the soil and to pick a relatively cool spot. In my case this is an area that is in light shade, close to a water feature that cools the area down with a light mist on hot days.

"[Blue Poppies] do well and are reasonably perennial in these conditions. This past season, however, was a flop, with only a few dozen flowers from a dozen plants and several deaths."

Fertile Blue Poppy hybrids (*M.* 'Lingholm') also have a fragile footing in the Lady Byng Garden at Rideau Hall, the Governor General's official residence in Ottawa. But three hundred miles (five hundred kilometres) farther east, on the south shore of the St. Lawrence River, flourishes one of the world's most famous stands of Himalayan Blue Poppies.

FOLLOWING PAGE 'Mrs. Jebb' sometimes wears extra petticoats.

The lake of Blue Poppies at
Les Jardins de Métis.

CHAPTER SIX

ELSIE'S EDEN

So well does it grow that to walk along a path between gently sloping
banks entirely veiled with the exquisite blue poppies
is like going through some ethereal valley in a land of dreams.

ELSIE REFORD[1]

LES JARDINS DE MÉTIS, OTHERWISE known as Reford Gardens, straddle the Mitis River where it flows into the St. Lawrence some 185 miles (three hundred kilometres) downstream from Quebec City. When Sir George Stephen, founder and president of the Canadian Pacific Railway, bought the land in the 1880s, creating a garden was the last thing on his mind. His aim was to secure the exclusive rights to fly-fish the huge spawning salmon that rested in the pools on their journey upriver. Among the expert anglers who spent much of the summer at Estevan Lodge, the "fishing camp" that Stephen built, was his niece, Elsie Reford. Uncle George made the property over to her in 1918. Perhaps it was Elsie's complete lack of horticultural training that enabled her to come up with the madcap scheme of building a great garden at Estevan. It was 1926. At fifty-four, she was well into middle age. There were scoffers, of course. Growing a garden in a wilderness spruce forest was unheard of—a fool's quest. Impossible in these parts where winters are brutal and only 110 days are free of frost.

Elsie Reford was resolute. Her workers made soil to build up the thin, acid clay, hauling gravel from the beach and peat, manure and leaf-mould from nearby farms.

She learned as she went, buying seeds and plants from England, corresponding with noted gardeners, in the process becoming herself a skilled and creative plantswoman. In 1929 she joined the Royal Horticultural Society and must have heard about Blue Poppy mania, the excitement generated by the display of plants grown from Frank Kingdon-Ward's seed. She ordered seed (which, happily for future generations of visitors to Les Jardins de Métis, must have arrived fresh) and by the mid-1930s, her Blue Poppies were established.

Some years later, Frank Kingdon-Ward wrote of receiving a letter "from a lady in Canada, enclosing a photograph showing hundreds of plants flowering in her garden on the shores of the St. Lawrence estuary."[2]

Today, Les Jardins de Métis are renowned for drifts of some ten thousand *Meconopsis betonicifolia*, planted in woodland glades, flowering in early July. These are the descendants of Elsie's plants and, given the very rudimentary state of Canadian gardening in the 1930s, she was certainly among the first to grow the Blue Poppy in this country.

This extraordinary achievement owes its success to Elsie's perseverance and flair, encouraged by a microclimate that well suits the Blue Poppies. In winter, deep snow protects the resting crowns. In summer, mists and rain are common, as cooling air streams up from the tidal estuary, which here is over thirty miles (fifty kilometres) from shore to shore.

Elsie Reford gardened at Estevan into her eighties, hunting through catalogues in her quest for new species or varieties to add to her collection, particularly peonies and lilies, which she loved. She ordered masses of plants, always ready to try something new, such as the wide, blue borders planted exclusively with hundreds of gentians. A team of gardeners was kept busy under her close direction, bringing her projects to life.

Elsie died at ninety-five in 1967, ten years after she gave Estevan and the gardens to her son. He sold to the Quebec government in 1961 and Les Jardins

The Blue Poppy—deferential and demure.

de Métis became a public attraction, as they are to this day. In 1994 the government's plan to privatize the gardens came to the attention of Elsie's great-grandson, Alexander Reford, a young Oxford-trained historian. He put together a non-profit consortium, Les Amis des Jardins de Métis, which won the bid. Alexander resigned his academic position at the University of Toronto to become director of the gardens. Like Elsie, he brought with him no horticultural experience.

In tribute to his great-grandmother, Alexander Reford is revitalizing and restoring Elsie's garden just as she would have wished. He refers to her detailed garden journal, and his great-grandfather's black-and-white photographs of the garden as it evolved. The informality of the gardens and the very brief summer flowering season bring everything into bloom at once. Great swaths of peonies mingle with roses, spires of delphiniums and towering lilies in a uniquely exuberant explosion of colour and scent, while the massed heavenly blue of ten thousand Blue Poppies forms perhaps the largest cultivated congregation in the world.

❋ ❋ ❋

Early one July, when Rosemary and I visited Les Jardins de Métis, our own Blue Poppies were already reduced to bundles of ragged stalks, topped with seed capsules ripening in the sun. At Les Jardins, it was show time. Picture a shaded glade of several thousand pampered poppies, all but a few stoutly perennial, standing shoulder to shoulder in a foot (thirty centimetres) of black, crumbly leaf-mould. That's Blue Poppy Heaven.

How, I wondered, would Frank Kingdon-Ward have described the spectacle? His writing is awash in watery images: Flowers "toss like white sea foam on a choppy ocean of dark green foliage."[3] Rhododendrons are "heather-purple seas,"[4] "mahogany seas,"[5] "sulphur seas,"[6] "ruffled seas, with a pink foam of blossom frothing over."[7] "A stream of Blue Poppies ..."[8] In choosing the metaphor to paint this throng of *Meconopsis betonicifolia*, he would likely have been equally florid, though I think he might have come up with something less action-packed in order to convey the tranquility of the scene, the *stillness*. A *lake*. Yes: a lake of blue, its surface barely rippled by eddies of cooling air, rising from the St. Lawrence River below.

A historic collection of sky-blue
flowers, much like the wild
ones described by Frank
Kingdon-Ward.

To Kingdon-Ward, this lake of Blue Poppies, growing in splendid isolation well away from the main gardens, would have looked familiar—reminiscent of the wild Tibetan Poppy. For these plants, being descendants of those that Elsie started in the 1930s, are probably not far removed from the wild seed gathered by Kingdon-Ward in the course of his 1924 expedition with Lord Cawdor.

Close inspection bore this out. The flowers were uniformly the colour of a summer's day—azure-blue, just as described in the field by Kingdon-Ward, rather than the richer, more saturated, drop-dead blue of contemporary examples of the species, which have been selected and re-selected over decades of cultivation. Most had just four petals, a few five or six, but there were no doubles and no ruinous purple. The plants, sheltered in the dappled shade of forty-year-old pines, were identical in leaf and stem, consistent in height and formation, strongly suggesting derivation from a single seed lot. It seemed

As in Elsie's day, white martagon lilies make cool companions.

we were looking at a population of Blue Poppies that was stranded in time, with no new blood added to the gene pool for some seventy-five years. In cultivation, this is rare, if not unique. This is a historic collection.

If happiness can be ascribed to meconopsis, these were positively purring in response to the watchful ministrations of the gardeners, who take pride in tending the plants as if they were their own. They give the same care to much smaller patches of *M. betonicifolia* in the main areas of Les Jardins de Métis, where, as in Elsie's day, they share space with white turkscap lilies (*Lilium martagon* var. *album*). This harmonious pairing would strike a false note in the Pacific Northwest, where the poppies are done for before the martagons bloom. In keeping with Elsie's enthusiasm for trying the new, the head gardener, Patricia Gallant, is eager to expand the Asiatic poppy collection, starting with *MM.* 'Lingholm' and *punicea*, the Red Poppywort. Furthermore, their meconopsis expert, Jean-Yves Roy, has ventured into Blue Poppy missionary work, founding small experimental colonies of *M. betonicifolia* in various other regions of Quebec.

The Blue Poppy is the emblem of Les Jardins, but there's much, much more to these lovely stroll gardens, which, in their informality (please *do* walk on the grass), have the air of a private garden. And of course they are: Elsie's private garden. Elsie would be happy with her great-grandson's stewardship. In a sense, she's still around. For here and there, small, pretend telescopes, mounted on tripods, are focussed on a particular spot. Take a peek: there's the chatelaine of Estevan, perhaps sitting on a bench, perhaps picking flowers for the dining table at the lodge—Elsie, informally captured in sepia photographs taken by her husband over half a century ago—linking the past with the present.

M. betonicifolia; a glimpse of blue stocking through a slit skirt.

A single plant lacks *oomph*.
They really should be planted *en masse*.

CHAPTER SEVEN

GET GROWING

I don't believe I have special talents.
I have persistence.
After the first failure, second failure,
third failure, I kept trying.

CARLO RUBBIA[1]

IF YOU CAN FIND A garden centre that sells Himalayan Blue Poppies, don't buy just one or two. A single plant lacks *oomph*, like a one-girl chorus line. Commercially grown meconopsis are likely to be expensive at best, larcenously over-priced at worst. Sometimes the foliage is soft, the plants having been force-fed to bring them to market. There's a pretty good chance they may die over the winter. Or they may die after flowering, leaving you where you started— poppyless. However, should you nevertheless buy ready-to-plant poppies, and should you have survivors breaking the surface with their hairy noses in spring, and should you have a bloom or two—well, let the seed ripen and try to grow your own. For, unless you're happy to make a substantial annual investment in new plants, this is the only way to maintain a display of Blue Poppies. They really should be planted *en masse*.

Blue Poppies in the garden will occasionally seed themselves if you leave the surrounding soil undisturbed, but this is trusting matters to the whims of fickle nature. The prospect of success will be greater by far if you take charge and raise plants from seed under carefully controlled conditions. First, the ingredients:

- ✓ Fresh seed
- ✓ Sterile, peat-based compost
- ✓ Clean, plastic containers
- ✓ Temperature between 8° and 20°C
- ✓ Water, light, air
- ✓ A modicum of patience
- ✓ A dash of hope

First obtain seed—fresh seed. A good source is one of the seed exchanges run by horticultural societies for their members. These are usually reliable, but the portions are often niggardly. Best of all, cultivate the acquaintance of someone who grows the Blue Poppy and scrounge a ripe seed capsule in summer. As a last resort, steal one. Press: it should be firm if filled with good seed. A skinny pod that feels soft may be filled with infertile dust, aborted seed that has not developed. One plump pod is all you need to start your own meconopsis glade. I'm sure Elsie Reford began with no more.

The pod must ripen on the plant, while the seed fuels up with all the nutrients necessary to carry it through germination and early life. The pod is ready to harvest when its stem has dried and turned brown, or when "dehiscing"—the capsule splitting along the seams—has started. Spread the seed on a piece of paper and let it stand in a dry place indoors, out of the sun, for a few days. Then, package the seed, label it and store it in a dry part of your fridge. Wait for cool weather before sowing.

All seeds need moisture, warmth and air to germinate. Meconopsis seeds also need light, and they require night temperatures below 15°C. (Compost is obviously necessary to hold the plant up, but not essential for germination.) Regardless of the

With fresh seed, success with M. 'Lingholm' is within the reach of any resolute gardener.

time of year you choose to start seed, do not use soil from your garden or from your compost heap, laden with happy red wrigglies, unless you fancy stinking up the kitchen while you boil it up in large pots to rid it of pests and diseases. Sterilizing in the microwave is equally unsavoury. A commercial, sterilized, soil-less, peat-based compost should be used. These are sold under various trade names—Sunshine mix, Pro mix, John Innes, Fisons. I buy Sunshine #1 and add about 25 per cent by volume of perlite or equivalent coarse grit to make sure there's good drainage and plenty of air pockets for the seedling roots to run about in. You can use Sunshine #4 and hold the additional grit.

Many garden books recommend sowing the Blue Poppy in early fall. The seed is fresh and germination should be good. Fill the container with tamped-down, moist compost. When squeezed it should tend to clump but not drip. No fertilizer should be added at this stage. Scatter the seeds lightly over the surface and press gently to ensure good contact. To help conserve surface moisture, a thin coat of fine vermiculite may be sprinkled on top. Mist the seeds and leave outside, sheltered from sun and rain. A shady cold frame is suitable, or under the eaves on the north side of the house. Don't let the pot dry out. If the weather is warm enough, germination will start in about three weeks; if not, the seedlings may not break the surface till late winter.

Some mistakes commonly made with a fall start:

- Using too small a container. A large container, such as a square, two-litre (half-gallon) pot, will not dry out too fast.

- Too little water. The seeds and resulting seedlings must never dry out. Moisten regularly with a soft, fine spray.

- Exposure to rain. This can wash out the seeds.

- Sowing too densely. More is not better. Crowded seedlings will be more susceptible to disease and will have to be thinned with tweezers.

- Slugs. Slugs. Slugs. Absolutely deadly. Like Napoleon's army, they march on their stomachs. A single slithering gastropod will polish off a pot of new sprouts at one sitting. Protect with a moat, by standing the pot on a brick in a shallow container filled with water.

- Exposure to hot sun. R.I.P.

- The problem with a fall start is this: whether or not the seedlings are transplanted before winter, and even if they're kept in a cold frame, many of the tiny plants will die before spring. At least, that's been my experience in the Pacific Northwest. For this reason I've abandoned fall sowing. I do better getting started in late winter, any time from early February till late March.

Usually around the middle of February I start the Blue Poppies indoors, where light, moisture and temperature can be controlled. Light is provided by a rack of cool fluorescent lights, the standard and inexpensive four-foot, two-tube unit that can be bought at a hardware or lighting store. Ordinary fluorescent tubes will do. I've found that special "grow lights" with their pink glow and "sunlight spectrum," at about four times the price, are no more effective for bringing on germination and keeping newly hatched seedlings in good health. A timer is connected to create twelve-hour days followed by twelve-hour nights.

Moisture is provided by a small, hand-pumped sprayer. A fine, soft spray will not disturb the seeds. The compost must not dry out, but over-watering should also be avoided. Some suggest covering the seeds with plastic wrap to hold mois-ture and maintain high humidity. In the case of meconopsis this could be fatal. Good air circulation contributes to good health. Excessive humidity contributes to damping off, the fungal scourge of seedlings.

I set up shop in a basement room. At night, when the lights are off, the area cools to 13°C. By day, the lights warm the surface to 20°C. Failing a suitable room in the house, I'd use the garage, with a source of regulated heat to prevent the temperature falling below 8°C.

If you wait for the spring equinox, when daylight is brighter and longer, natural-light options are possible. For example, you could start seed on a bright windowsill, though not in direct sun. Alternatively, you might try a shady part of

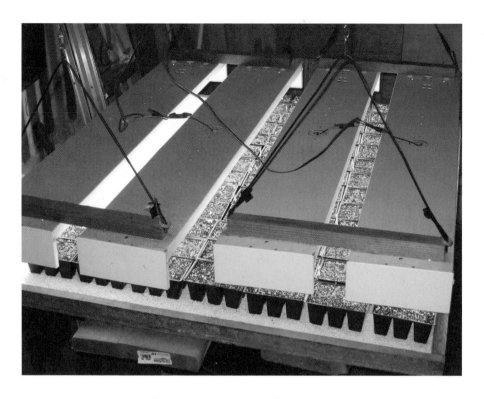

Starting indoors under lights.

a cool greenhouse, with standby warmth for possible frosty nights and ventilation in case the early spring sun overheats the space within and cooks the seedlings. But I much prefer to start the Blue Poppies earlier, to give them a head start on reaching planting-out size in early summer.

For indoor growing, I like to use the flimsy, six-pack plastic containers sold in many garden centres. (The sort of thing nurseries use for selling annual bedding plants.) These should be new or, if not, well-washed in a bleach solution. Sow the seeds on the surface as described for a fall start, topping off with a thin dressing of fine vermiculite. Be sparing. Gardeners tend to be overly generous when starting seed. This is not a good idea, because crowded seeds produce impoverished

Germination starts in about three weeks. The
seedlings on the left are showing the first true leaves.

seedlings, vulnerable to the dreaded damp off. If your seed is good, you can count
on over 50 per cent germination. Finally, mist and place the container under the
fluorescent tubes, which should hang about two inches (five centimetres) above
the surface.

Keep the compost moist with daily overhead misting and, all being well, your
Blue Poppies will start their perilous life after about three weeks. An advantage
of sterilized compost is that if anything comes up, it will be what you put in. The
first sign is a green shoot, often topped with a black seed casing. Soon, the casing
is pushed off and the shoot resolves itself into two seed leaves, the cotyledon. If
numerous shoots emerge in a cell, take tweezers and cull them to no more than five

well-spaced seedlings. Next, a hairy, true leaf will appear. When two true leaves are visible, roughly ten weeks after sowing, the plants, though still very tiny, are ready for transplanting. But first, they must be hardened off.

Hardening off is the process of acclimatizing the seedlings to outdoor conditions. If not gradually accustomed, they may be set back or die from the shock of sudden temperature change. During the day, move the containers outside, sheltered from rain and sun. Bring them back in overnight if the temperature is predicted to fall below 5°C. And out again in the morning. After a few days of this, the tiny plants should be well adjusted and can be safely left outside, even during cool nights. However, if you live in an area liable to late spring frosts, some pro-tection would be a sensible precaution. And don't forget the slugs. Tender young Blue Poppies are choice cuts for these mucus-trailing molluscs.

Now that the seedlings have two true leaves and are about half an inch (1.3 centimetres) across, they may be

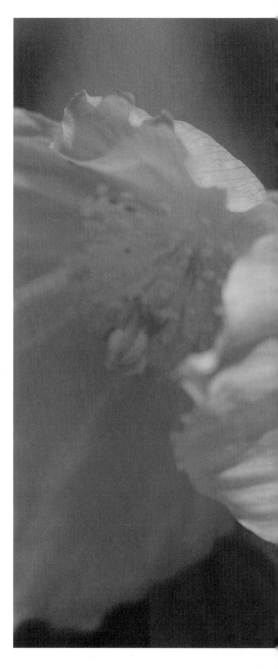

M. betonicifolia var. *alba*. This cream-centred variation originated in our garden.

transplanted. Here's where I find the six-pack containers most useful, because the contents of a single cell can be emptied, leaving the other five undisturbed, for further growth if necessary. First, line up several four-inch (ten-centimetre) plastic pots and loosely fill them with the same peat-based, gritty compost. Use your finger to make a deep hole in the centre of each. Now, select one of the cells and carefully tip out the seedlings and all the compost. Next, holding the seedlings by a seed leaf (the cotyledon), carefully tease the plants apart. Do not handle the roots or stem. If some compost adheres, so much the better. Then, lower the fledgling into the hole you made in its new home and very gently firm the compost. Add more compost as needed, so that the transplant sits at the same level as it did in the six-pack. One plant per pot. Finally, water in with a dilute solution of a root-stimulating fertilizer. These are sold under such names as Plant Starter or Upstart and always have a high middle number—e.g., 10–50–10 or 5–15–5. As a last touch, I sprinkle a pinch of slow-release fertilizer around each plant. With due care, 90 per cent survival can be expected.

Now the transplants are left outside to grow on—still sheltered from rain and midday sun. They will sit and sulk for two or three weeks and some may die. This is normal. Then the survivors start to grow as the weather warms up and the roots explore. Throughout, you must keep a close eye on the babies, keeping them cool and moist. And, particularly, you must stand sentry against a sneak slug attack. For Blue Poppies are a lip-smacking, mouth-watering, eye-popping, finger-snapping, toe-tapping, rib-tickling, gustatory delight for these torpid lower echelons of life. The hairy leaves merely tickle their tummies as they go about their nocturnal business of rasping the rosettes to the ground. The rasp is the tongue, armed with cross rows of small, horny teeth.

With a February start, by mid-July the Blue Poppies will have filled the pots. The trademark hairy foliage now forms a rosette, with leaves at least four inches (ten centimetres) long. They're ready to plant. The earlier this is done, the larger the poppy will grow before winter shuts it down, much improving the prospect of flowers the following spring.

Choose a place in the garden, ideally in deciduous shade or a spot in open shade, such as the north side of the house—a cool, quiet site, sheltered from afternoon sun and strong winds. Meconopsis will perform poorly in total shade and hardly at all in soil invaded by the roots of cedar trees.

To prepare the bed, dig well, dig deeply, dig to a foot or more and generously invigorate the soil with moisture-retentive, coarse compost and manure. Mound it up if you like. If your soil is heavy in clay, it may prove necessary to replace it or at least work in plenty of humus. Perfect drainage is essential and acid soil is required.

Blue Poppies should be set out in groups for best effect, planted about a foot apart. They are gluttons and will not bloom if under-fed. So I muddle in a little all-purpose fertilizer in each hole, as well as a double fistful of well-rotted manure (anything other than mushroom or rabbit manure) to feed the roots. Finally, I scatter a fat pinch of slow-release pellets on the surface. And don't forget the slugs. Or the snails. At this stage the juicy leaves are a delicacy much fancied by these surprisingly fastidious invertebrates. An effective defence must be mounted. Young Blue

Alkaline soil will not harm the plants, but it will affect the flowering colour. For this reason, mushroom manure must not be used. It's high in lime. Also shun rabbit poop. These creatures are often fed alfalfa, which is calcium-rich and therefore alkaline.

The chemistry is explained by Jennifer Schultz Nelson, of the University of Illinois: "The Himalayan Blue Poppy is one of the few true blue flowers in the world. ... The blue color is provided by the pigment delphinidin, named for being originally isolated from Delphinium. For the delphinidin in the flower to appear blue, the environment inside the plant's cells must be acidic. The soil provides this acid, otherwise the flowers appear pinkish-purple. This 'acid factor' is what makes blue such a rare find in the plant kingdom. Not only does a plant have to have the gene to make delphinidin in its flower cells, it must also be able to maintain a level of acidity within the cell to make the pigment appear blue. Few plants can accomplish this."[2] •

Blue Poppies should be set out
in groups for best effect.

Poppy plants are also liable to suffer rapid decline and death from excessive heat, especially dry heat, even if the roots are well watered. Temperatures in the 30°C range are certainly dangerous to their health and potentially fatal unless the plants are enveloped in a cooling mist. If these hazards can be avoided, and if the ground is well prepared, considerable growth will be put on through late summer and early fall, building strength and improving the prospects for flowers the following spring.

By Christmas, the leaves have withered and the plant's energy is stored in a resting bud just beneath the surface. Other than the label, no sign remains that a Blue Poppy waits for spring. No protection from frost is needed.

Then follows a season of suspense. The plant winters, in wait for warmth to trigger growth anew. The gardener winters, in a state of some apprehension and anxiety. Will this poppy reappear? Suspense in both senses is lifted when, in early spring, like the tips of a kitten's ears, the first bristly leaf points appear. Or not. Crown rot is another common cause of sudden death for meconopsis, the result of sodden soil.

If all the poppies you planted in summer emerge in the spring, count yourself a master gardener. If all the poppies emerge *and* bloom, count yourself a grandmaster gardener. However, as we shall see, if all the poppies emerge and you *let* them bloom in the year after seeding, you are likely to suffer long-term pain as the price of short-term gain.

CHAPTER EIGHT

KEEPING UP APPEARANCES

I have one share in corporate Earth,
and I am nervous about the management.

E.B. WHITE¹

I'M OFTEN ASKED IF BLUE POPPIES stand a better chance of becoming perennial if the flowering stems are cut off at an early stage, sacrificing the first year of flowering as an investment in long-term survival. The assumption is that rather than eagerly flowering itself to death, the poppy will spend its resources on building more crowns, with a more robust supporting root structure. Many nursery catalogues and garden writers advise this strategy. My experience suggests this is true—particularly if the poppy puts forth a flowering shoot in the year after seeding, which it usually will do in the Pacific Northwest, if well grown. But I don't do it. I can't bear to.

After all the loving care I've invested in raising the things, I'm not about to deprive myself of the pleasure of the blue flowers in the largest possible numbers at the earliest possible opportunity. To me whacking the stem would be as distressing as culling a litter of new-born puppies, and I've never done that either. Whether or not deflowering makes a difference, I believe that heredity plays a part:

M. betonicifolia displays its distinctively
frilly skirts.

that some Blue Poppies in a batch of seed are programmed to be perennial and some are programmed to be *monocarpic* (once fruiting), that is, to die after flowering, whenever that happens. I take out insurance, each year growing from seed all the replacements I'm likely to need, with plenty left over to share with gardening friends. And I always collect seed only from the finest established perennials.

One of the reasons that Blue Poppies are scarce in cultivation is that they tend to be short-lived. It's not a plant, like the Lenten rose for example, that you can stick in the ground and expect to last a lifetime. Many factors determine its lifespan—the care you offer, the growing conditions, the weather, heredity—but even with the most tender loving care, in the Pacific Northwest we have to be prepared for eventual loss.

At the time of flowering, or soon after, the plants will let you know whether or not they're planning to stick around for another year. Fresh new leaves, growing from new crowns, appear around the base of the old stem. If not, the plant is finished. Away with it to the compost pile.

Over time, unless the soil is replenished, the Blue Poppies will lose their edge in performance, dwindling to strung-out weaklings, eventually too weary to put out a flower, and without flowers the plants are of little worth. Preventive measures begin with a late-spring top-dressing of coarse organic matter, preferably every year. This adds nourishment, while also conserving moisture and helping to regulate the temperature at the roots in hot weather. Leaf-mould, garden compost and manure are all suitable. (But remember: no mushroom manure or rabbit poop.) Take care to avoid burying the crowns.

Then, to improve the chances of a long and vigorous life, every three or four years the bed will need a complete overhaul. Some experienced Blue Poppy growers suggest doing this in early spring as the young shoots first break surface. I prefer summer, just after seed collection, allowing the disturbed plants time to recover and gain strength before winter puts a stop to further growth. Dig up the poppies with a large garden fork. Divide big clumps in two or more. Turn the bed over to a foot deep, incorporating plenty of fresh compost and manure. Replant. Water well. Mulch. Stand back. Admire. Look forward to another rhapsody in blue, year after year after year.

✻ ✻ ✻

If, as at Les Jardins de Métis, there's an acreage of deciduous woodland, what could be more lovely than unaccompanied drifts of *Meconopsis betonicifolia*? But if, like most of us, you have limited garden space and a desire to grow other beauties, no plants are better suited as bedfellows for the Blue Poppy than the candelabra primulas. Their architecture is the perfect complement.

Candelabra primulas are misnamed, insofar as the name suggests a branching plant. In fact, each crown of this primula race puts forth a single flowering stalk, a spike, bearing several tiered whorls of tightly clustered, five-petalled flowers. Like the Blue Poppy, the stalk, which may be as much as thirty inches (seventy-five centimetres) tall, erupts from a basal rosette of long, more-or-less oblong leaves. Like the Blue Poppy, the rosette remains bright and green until late fall, emerging again in early spring.

Most of the candelabra primulas are hardy perennials and will be very much at home in conditions that suit meconopsis well. If the Blue Poppies are healthy and happy in their situation, enjoying well-drained soil, rich in organic matter, with shelter from afternoon sun, the candelabra primulas will be healthy and happy, too, even though some are bog plants, accustomed to wet feet. Some of these primulas can be found in the alpine meadows of the Himalayas, growing in company with meconopsis.

Candelabra primulas grow in every primary hue *except* blue. Their flowering season overlaps the poppies. White, yellow, purple, red, orange and yellow, orchestrated with blue, may sound like a cacophony of colour. It could be, but as mentioned, the similarity in the architecture of Blue Poppies and candelabra primulas ties it all together. The colour combination certainly would not work if the poppies were bedfellows with, say, petunias, geraniums or tulips.

Candelabra species are seldom found in garden centres, either as plants or as seed, but it should be possible to order seed from several on-line catalogues, as well as from lists available to members of organizations such as the Alpine Garden Club of British Columbia, or Britain's Royal Horticultural Society. Candelabra primulas are easy to start from seed, following the methods described in the previous chapter for meconopsis. They should bloom in the

second year and thereafter form neat, long-lasting clumps.

Here are nine easily grown primulas:

- *P. anisidora* is a very fragrant plant, bearing brownish-purple flowers and anise-scented leaves. It grows to about eighteen inches (forty-five centimetres).

- *P. beesiana* has rose-pink flowers and stands two feet (sixty centimetres) tall.

- *P. bulleyana* was named for A. K. Bulley, the seedsman and famed primula collector who helped fund some of Frank Kingdon-Ward's expeditions. This species has deep orange flowers and grows somewhat taller than *P. beesiana*. These two species have been crossed and a rainbow range of colours can be obtained from seed

HERE AND FOLLOWING PAGES
Poppies and candelabra primulas make fine bedfellows, and bloom in a rainbow range of colours.

91

listed as *Primula × bullesiana*, a strain blooming in shades of cream to orange, pink to crimson, or purple or lilac.

- *P. burmanica* is a much smaller candelabra, having reddish-purple flowers with a yellow eye.

- *P. chungensis* is a hardy perennial, about two feet (sixty centimetres) tall, flowering in late spring with whorls of pale orange.

- *P. helodoxa* is a cheery, bright-yellow species, native to China. It's sweetly fragrant and can grow to three feet (ninety centimetres), flowering in early summer.

- *P. japonica*, as the name suggests, originates in Japan. It's a robust, woodland candelabra of average height that, once established, should never need to be started again, for it seeds itself generously. This is the candelabra most likely to be available in garden centres. Several varieties are in cultivation, with flowers in white, apricot-pink and crimson.

- *P. poissonii* from China is a small candelabra with tiered whorls of yellow-eyed, purple flowers.

- *P. pulverulenta* is among the tallest—up to three feet (ninety centimetres) —and most vigorous candelabra species. It has deep-red flowers and, like *P. japonica*, is very easy to grow, tolerating both sun and shade. The stems appear to have been lightly dusted with flour (appropriately, the botanical term is *farina*), an embellishment that graces many primulas. Recently, *P. pulverulenta* has been crossed with *P. chungensis* to produce *P. × chunglenta*—a lovely pink candelabra primula.

All these species provide a sublime accompaniment, as does the giant Himalayan cowslip, *Primula florindae*, which was introduced by Frank Kingdon-Ward and named in honour of his first wife, Florinda. He also named for her a rare,

The candelabra primula, 'Inverewe', is a rarity. It's named
for the famous garden in Scotland, where it originated

dwarf, yellow woodland poppy, *Meconopsis florindae*. It's not in cultivation.

Like the Blue Poppies, candelabra primulas will go dormant and vanish entirely for the winter, leaving a blank canvas, which may demand a few brush strokes to maintain interest. A small, slow-growing deciduous tree with appealing bark and shapely structure will do, such as the Japanese stewartia (*Stewartia pseudocamellia*). In addition, I like to paint-in the background with groups of the statuesque Satin Poppy, a particularly tall meconopsis with large rosettes that remain green throughout the year. This and other cousins of the Blue Poppy will be described in the next chapter.

The Rainbow Collection. For an eye-catching background, the stately Satin Poppy in full sail.

CHAPTER NINE

THE RAINBOW COLLECTION

Meconopsis ...
show in perfect purity all the colours imaginable.

JAMES COBB[1]

NOW, IN OUR GARDEN I grow all the Asiatic poppies I can. I am limited by sources of seed, which in turn are limited by the number of species in cultivation. For some, such as the rare and highly desirable dwarf poppy *Meconopsis bella* (surely worth growing for the name alone) are so precisely tuned to their Himalayan niche that they have never been successfully maintained beyond a year or two in captivity, despite several attempts over the last century.

I am limited also by the customary pattern of the Pacific Coast climate, which reliably delivers too warm, too dry summers alternating with sodden winters, the reverse of the dry winters and wet summers the poppies generally experience in their home and native land. We are saved, in part at least, by the connecting seasons: the almost-five-month-long spring, moist and cool, then gentle autumn, a benign segue into winter.

Finally, I am limited by my own skill and know-how. Although successful in germinating another rare dwarf, the imperial purple *M. delavayi*, and successful for

M. punicea unfurls like a butterfly
emerging from its cocoon.

the most part in transplanting it, I sadly watch the seedlings sigh and die after a few weeks or months—like Sudden Infant Death syndrome. Inexplicable. It's trial and error. Mostly error. Still, as Samuel Beckett advised:

No matter

Try again

Fail again

Fail better[2]

Earlier, we met the exquisite *M. punicea* in the wild. It is a poppy to shout and sing about, first flowering in Britain in 1904 from seed collected by Ernest Henry Wilson. In cultivation today in the botanic garden at Tromso, Norway, it seeds itself with abandon. Here in the Pacific Northwest, as a challenge I would classify it extreme.

- First, I have found it to be very difficult to germinate, seemingly requiring frost to break dormancy. The trouble is, we get very little frost. I sow the seed in a pot in the fall and leave it out all winter, sheltered from rain. With luck I may find a very few tiny sprouts emerging in late winter. I coddle them and check their health every day, shielding them from too much rain or sun. Most often there's nothing.

- Second, survivors are transplanted with the utmost care into small, four-inch (ten-centimetre) plastic pots, fed and watched over. And yet in this shifting climate the lives of healthy seedlings are often mysteriously cut short. SIDS again. For no reason I can fathom, plants just shrivel and expire.

- Third, any survivors are ready in late summer to be put out in the garden. Control of moisture continues to be important. And at this stage they're particularly vulnerable to destruction by slugs. An alternative and tempting fatal attraction must be offered.

M. punicea always looks as if its petals need ironing.

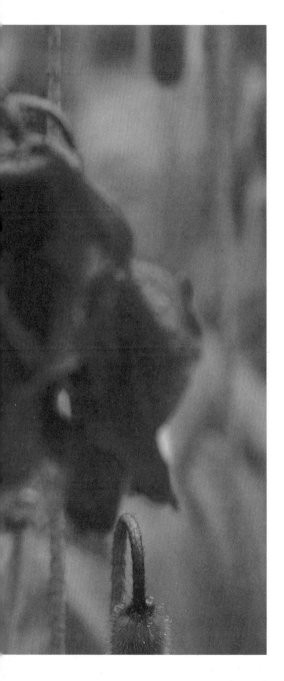

- Fourth, the leaves die and the plant winters as a tiny, grey-green button. The prospects for pulling the poppy through the Pacific Northwest season of heavy rains are improved with the overhead protection of a small plastic tent. As days lengthen toward the spring equinox, this button expands, a rosette of new, hairy leaves forms, and eventually buds appear. Then in April the thrill of the first flower, the first of several, each borne singly atop a slender stem up to eighteen inches (forty-five centimetres) tall. It blooms. Then it dies.

The hazards and trials faced by *M. punicea*, running the gauntlet from seed to bloom, are such that I managed to bring a plant or two to flower only twice in the first five years of trying.

The naughty bits are so deeply sheathed that hand pollination is required.

These put on a brave show, flowering themselves to death, *sometimes* leaving me with seed for another try. *Sometimes*, because without human intervention fertilization is unreliable. The flower's sexual parts are so deeply sheathed within the long, pendant petals that insects may not find them. It's necessary to make like a bee, using a soft brush or Q-tip to transfer pollen from stamens to stigma, or else flipping back the petals of two blooms and rubbing the naughty bits together. Without this assistance the seed pods may be entirely or partially filled with dust—undeveloped seed.

I cherish this eloquent vermilion poppy all the more for its elusiveness. And it's not even blue.

Closely related and even more difficult to germinate is *M. quintuplinervia*. Among the smallest of the meconopsis tribe, it's a charming perennial, with lavender-coloured flowers. Reginald Farrer, who is credited with its introduction, was especially fond of this species, which he dubbed the Harebell Poppy. Once he came across an albino variation, "as white and clean and clear as the soul of St. John."[3]

Tight rosettes of leaves form and spread across the ground when the Harebell Poppy is happy. Once established, it's supposed to be easy to keep going and readily propagated by division. So I thought it was doing well in my garden after it flowered nicely one spring and multiplied modestly. But winter rains carried it off. Another small clump, imported from Scotland, silently faded away in its first encounter with a Pacific summer. To add to the difficulty, seed is in very short supply because the Harebell Poppy is reluctant to produce any.

The two species, *M. punicea* and the Harebell Poppy, are the parents of *M. × cookei*, which occurs naturally, though uncommonly, in the alpine meadows of China. In nature, observers have dismissed its colour as a murky magenta, the ugly offspring of comely parents. However, Leslie Drummond, who gardens in Scotland (we'll meet him later), recreated the cross in 1996 and produced the lovely 'Old Rose' hybrid. I have this plant and I take the greatest care of it. It's probably

Farrer's Harebell Poppy.

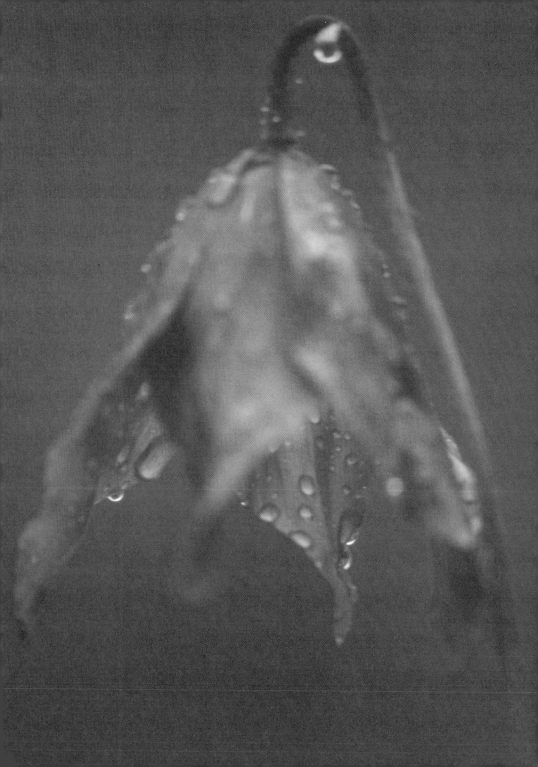

the only specimen in Canada and the most precious plant in my garden, encircled with a strip of copper sheeting to keep out slugs and over-wintered under a cloche to shelter the dormant crowns from drenching storms. I have cosseted it safely through several winters, but it refuses to spread here, as it will do most readily in more suitable conditions.

M. × cookei is perennial and usually sterile. It vanishes entirely in November and I hold my breath till March, when I'm greatly relieved to see the fuzzy tips of new leaves emerging. 'Old Rose' has lived to bloom again.

Most of the Asiatic poppy species, unlike the illustrious big blues, are monocarpic—once fruiting. That is to say, they die after flowering. This does not necessarily mean they are biennial plants, because many, especially the evergreen species, may sit for years before blooming and dying.

Among the easiest of these evergreens to grow is the Satin Poppy, the name commonly given to *Meconopsis napaulensis,* one of the first species to be introduced to cultivation, possibly as early as 1831. This is a stately plant, which, in ideal conditions, can produce a towering, flowering spike eight feet (2.5 metres) tall, hung with scores of four-inch (ten centimetre), red to purple blooms, rarely white, on short stalks. In spring, this magnificent array bursts from the centre of an evergreen rosette, which itself can reach three feet (ninety centimetres) across after three or more years. The Satin Poppy flowers, sets seed and dies, its task in the order of things fulfilled. That is the way with monocarps.

There are two other, equally statuesque and easy-to-grow, evergreen Asiatic poppy species: *M. paniculata* and *M. regia,* both in shades of yellow. The former, found across the Himalayas, has been in cultivation since the mid-nineteenth century. *M. regia,* native to central Nepal, was a late-comer to gardens, in 1931, and lost no time in practising miscegenation with its close kin: *MM. napaulensis* and *paniculata.* These three species live apart in the wild, but in gardens they breed just as readily with each other as with their own kind.

M. × cookei 'Old Rose' is the most precious plant in my garden.

NICOLAI MIKHAILOVICH PRZEWALSKI

Among the dauntless heroes whose exploits contributed to the discovery of the Asiatic poppies, Major-General N. M. Przewalski (1839–1888) must be counted. In pictures he looks like the template for Joseph Stalin: thick, dark hair brushed straight back; a massive moustache; resolute chin; cool, clear eyes focussed on some distant vision. He's decked out in the gold braid of an officer in the Imperial Russian Army.

Educated in botany and zoology, General Przewalski made important collections in the fields of both flora and fauna. But he was by profession a geographer, and, in the service of Czar Alexander III, he made a series of great exploratory journeys south from Siberia across the deserts and mountain ranges of Central Asia, accompanied by a small detachment of Cossacks. His goal was to reach Lhasa, the capital of Tibet.

During the first journey, from 1870 to 1873, he captured a wild pony in the Altai Mountains of Mongolia, a small, dun-coloured animal that he recognized as a new species. Przewalski's horse, *Equus caballus przewalski*, as it was later named, became extinct in the wild by 1960, thanks largely to competition from domesticated ruminants. However, animals bred in European zoos have recently been reintroduced.

During the second journey, 1876 to 1877, Przewalski discovered the Altun mountain range and rediscovered Lop Nur, a lake in the heart of Asia not visited by any European since Marco Polo.

During the third journey, 1879 to 1880, Przewalski came within 160 miles (260 kilometres) of Lhasa before being turned back by Tibetan officials, the lamas.

During the fourth journey, 1883 to 1885, accompanied by a taxidermist and a detachment of Cossacks, he discovered three new Asiatic poppies, *Meconopsis integrifolia*, *M. punicea* and *M. quintuplinervia*.

During the fifth journey, which began in 1888, Nicolai Mikhailovich Przewalski incautiously drank unboiled water, contracted typhoid and died. He never did reach Lhasa. •

In the wild, each has its distinctive flower colour and leaf shape. In gardens there are flowers of cream and yellow, all shades of pink and red, and occasional bi-colours.

Depending on the mix of genes from the original species, the edges of the long, hairy leaves may vary in shape from almost smooth to deeply lobed or dissected. The leaves may be grey-green, blue-green, yellow-green or simply green. They're covered with fine hairs, often giving a shimmering golden, rufous or silvery dusting to the leaves and buds. In effect, cultivation has brought these three cousins together and made them kissing cousins, to the point where it's implausible to claim with confidence that any single plant is truly, purely and without any adulteration, any one of the three species. You can be sure it's a hybrid, unless you grew it from seed you know was collected in the wild. Suspect that plants sold as *Meconopsis napaulensis* or *regia* or *paniculata*—or indeed seed offered under these names— will be hybrids, not the species attributed. In fact, true *M. regia* is thought not to be in cultivation today.

No matter. Let's simply call these plants Satin Poppies (or *Meconopsis napaulensis* hybrids, if you prefer to be botanically correct) and enjoy their promiscuity and their infinite variety. A stand of Satin Poppies is a fine sight in late spring and the evergreen rosettes add colour to the winter garden, glittering with beads of dew suspended in the furry leaves. Just remember to save the seed from the best plants because they will all, inevitably, die after flowering.

I grow *M. wallichii*, named for Dr. Nathaniel Wallich, an early nineteenth-century polymath (surgeon, plant collector, botanical writer, founder of museums), who preserved seeds on the long voyage to England by packing them in brown sugar. Ever since this plant was first described in the 1880s, botanists and taxonomists have been unable to agree on its classification. The "lumpers" maintain it is a form of *M. napaulensis*, while the "splitters" insist it's a distinct species. Whatever, *M. wallichii* is another evergreen monocarp, with a five-foot (1.5-metre) spike of numerous small flowers, ranging in colour from white to washed-out blue to washed-out pinky-mauve. At least that is my experience, though from pictures I know the real thing can bear sky-blue flowers. The trouble is, once again, that this species (or variety if you're a lumper) has crossed and recrossed with compatible

The evergreen rosette of the Satin Poppy
adorns the garden through winter.

relatives, giving rise to a hodgepodge of pasty pastels at the blue end of the spectrum. It's therefore important not to pass on seed from inferior plants, a principle that should be observed for all garden-grown Asiatic poppies.

I've found this poppy easy to grow from seed listed in The Meconopsis Group's seed exchange, described by the donor as "*M. wallichii* blue form." The results have been very variable: some golden-haired, some green, some with fully dissected leaves, some less so. None have been more than faintly blue. This is the problem with seed exchanges. Too often the listings are not what they're cracked up to be. It's really not the organizer's fault. It's the contributor who, for instance, may have acquired and grown wrongly labelled seed and then sent in the resulting harvest with the same wrong name. This would explain why the *M. latifolia* I started last year transformed itself into *M. betonicifolia*. Or why seed implausibly marked *M. grandis alba* leafed out as *M. betonicifolia alba*.

It's a little hard to love *M. wallichii*. It's nowhere near the top of my list, at least not until I find the true-blue form at the end of the rainbow. It looks its best just as the buds are about to open, the gold-bristled stem silhouetted against the light. In bloom it starts to look scruffy as the foliage withers. Its singular contribution to the meconopsis collection is its habit of extending the poppy-flowering season by blooming in mid-summer.

M. superba, on the other hand, is a highly desirable poppy with a limited range on the border of Bhutan and Tibet, first introduced to gardens in the mid-1930s. Superb indeed: a thing of beauty with a silvery-green rosette brightening the winter garden and, eventually, in spring a four-foot (1.2 metres) spike of radiant, very large, white flowers.

Eventually. One thing I've learned about this species: it can take many years to bloom. I've lost count of the years I've been waiting for several plants

PAGES 112–113 The Satin Poppy. In gardens, the genes of at least three species have mingled to produce a range of colours (other than blue) in the tallest of poppies.

to come into flower, each spring peering into the deep nucleus of the rosette, watching for signs of an emerging flower spike. Waiting in vain, despite increasing bribes offered in the form of generous top dressing with manure and half a handful of slow-release fertilizer. And when at last it does flower, being monocarpic, it then dies. Unlike other evergreen species in my collection, *M. superba* will breed true. It is self-fertile and seed will germinate well if started in fall, within a few weeks of harvest.

Pygmy versions of these evergreen monocarpic poppies are *M. gracilipes* and the unpronounceable *M. dhwojii*, honouring Major Lal Dhwoj, who collected plants for the King of Nepal. These two, both from Nepal, were introduced around 1930. They're quite similar, both with deeply dissected leaves and a stem about two feet (sixty centimetres) tall, covered in golden hairs and bearing yellow, cup-shaped flowers. The true species are said to be charming; however, seed grown under these names is likely to result in, at best, a reasonable facsimile of the real thing. Like so many species discussed earlier, in gardens they've enjoyed years of undocumented hybridizing. Which is

ABOVE *M. napaulensis* hybrids flower in many
colours, and leaf out in shades of green and grey.
Save seed only from the finest forms.

LEFT *M. superba*—radiant white, with a
silvery-green winter rosette.

why, having grown them, I find them to be disappointingly homely.

In 1921 the first British Everest expedition, George Leigh Mallory's first encounter with the mountain, collected *Meconopsis horridula* at an astonishing 19,000 feet (5,800 metres), an elevation at which only the very toughest plants can hang on to life, cowering in crevices to find shelter from the howling winds and frigid temperatures, with only a few weeks free of snow. Here, this monocarpic species pins itself firmly in place with a long taproot. It produces a tiny rosette, from which pale-blue poppies bloom, raised on stems barely an inch off the ground. This high alpine form is very difficult to grow and is seldom, if ever, found in gardens.

In the meadows several thousand feet lower, the very variable *M. horridula* is dispersed throughout the Himalayas and beyond, appearing in diverse forms with flowers in a full range of blues and violet, occasionally white and, very rarely, pink or

The very variable *M. horridula*. Handle with gloves.

yellow. This poppy usually blooms as a biennial. It's quite easy to grow from seed but won't necessarily breed true. It took four years of starting seed billed as *M. horridula alba* before I finally produced a lovely, white-flowered plant. The horrid part refers to the tiny, sharp spines that cover the entire plant. It's sometimes called the "prickly blue poppy" or the "spiny meconopsis." Handle with gloves. Quite often this is a coarse species. There's a basal rosette with all the appeal of a hawkweed, a lank rosette of long, narrow leaves. There's a weak stem that seems too short and tends to flop about.

Frankly, it lacks charisma. But like the ugly duckling, it's transformed into a swan, at least for a week or two when the numerous flowers, clustered along the stem, open from the top down. It is then an exquisite thing, with two-inch (five-centimetre) blooms revealed in the purest shades of blue, with a cluster of buff-coloured anthers at the centre. The prickly blue poppy leaves no visible sign of its presence over winter, with the leaves decayed and the resting bud below the surface.

I have never grown a Yellow Chinese Poppy that matches the yellow splendour of the wild poppies I saw growing in a damp gully in western Sichuan. In cultivation, *M. integrifolia* first flowered in Paris in 1896 from seed sent from Sichuan by Abbé Farges, another of the French missionary plant collectors, but it was Chinese Wilson, collecting for Veitch in 1903, who first sent home enough for commercial exploitation. Reginald Farrer, the plant explorer who liked to coin simple, friendly names, called it the Lampshade Poppy. It lives up to its name, having the largest flower of any Asiatic poppy. In the wild, specimens have been measured at eleven inches (twenty-eight centimetres) across. Nor have I yet matched the wild form of *M. pseudointegrifolia*, its twelve-syllable sibling, which blooms in our garden as a ridiculously top-heavy plant, just a foot (thirty centimetres) tall, with a bowl-shaped, bright-yellow flower absurdly out of proportion to the supporting leafage. Frank Kingdon-Ward noted it growing

In the garden, the Lampshade Poppy does not match the yellow splendour of the wild form.

three times that height on his approach to the Tsangpo Gorges: "Tall and stately, these sulphur poppies are the most conspicuous objects on the moorland, looming above the other flowers like yellow moons."[4]

Here again, the splitters separate these two yellow species, while the lumpers insist they are merely variations on a theme. I grow both and they are not especially difficult, but they're reputed to be the greediest of all Asiatic poppies, so this year I shall feed the seedlings till they burst. Regular doses of 20–20–20. Then, when planting them out, I'll give them a deep hole with a shovelful of well-rotted steer manure worked in.

The Yellow Chinese Poppy, whether *M. integrifolia* or *pseudointegrifolia* (and I'm with the lumpers), retreats to a fuzzy button over winter. Then in March, a pleasing rosette of hairy, oblong leaves appears, with hints of pink and gold in the better forms. Both species flower as a biennial if well-grown. Then they die. There are said to be perennial forms of *M. integrifolia* and one day I hope one comes my way.

I would like to do better with *M. simplicifolia*, a Blue Poppy thought to have been one of the first of the Asiatic species to be raised in cultivation, in 1848. It exists in both perennial and monocarpic forms. In both, there's a basal rosette of strappy leaves with flowers arising from the centre on bare stems up to two feet (sixty centimetres) tall. The pity is that the sublime, sky-blue colouring usually occurs only in the monocarpic version.

This dainty poppy has been in gardens here and there for well over a century, though it's not widely grown and is overshadowed by the big blue perennials. Seeds are rarely available. Some came my way a few years ago and I started them in late winter. I got excellent germination, raised a dozen plants, set them out in the garden. This seemed easy. Too easy. One lonely poppy survived to bloom weakly in spring. I learned the hard way that this, of all Asiatic poppy species in cultivation,

M. pseudointegrifolia, with flowers of
the purest yellow, though in this instance,
absurdly top-heavy.

is found to be the most discontent with winter wet and may succumb to crown rot, even if the soil is well-drained. Protection from rain is essential. Forewarned is forearmed, so with another batch of seed from Scottish friends, I started again. Just one sprouted, grew, lived to face the winter wet and, suitably waterproofed, survived, flowered and died. Once again I learned the hard way; in this instance, that germination of *M. simplicifolia* is unpredictable. In the next experiment, I shall ask my friends to send the seed as soon as it ripens, and start the process in fall, wintering the seedlings in a cold frame. Trial and error. That is the way with meconopsis.

The latest addition to my repertoire is *M. aculeata*, a quite charming little chap that grows at heights from 8,000 to 14,000 feet (2,400 to 4,300 metres) in the westernmost range of the Asiatic poppies—as far west as Kashmir. (Kingdon-Ward called it "the prickly poppy of Kashmir."[5]) The climate there is hotter and drier, so, provided the roots are kept moist, it should be more tolerant of heat than other species.

This suggests *M. aculeata* might fare well in a sunny rock garden, if the tap root can be kept cool, mulched with gravel. I shall try that. It certainly would make an attractive rock garden plant, being small and tidy, with several two-inch (five-centimetre), frilly, robin's-egg-blue flowers along a very spiny twelve-inch (thirty-centimetre) stem. At least that describes the sweet poppy I grew from seed last year. Reportedly, the species varies considerably in height and colour (shades of purple to blue). Moreover, there may be several flowers on a single stem or a single flower on each of several stems. Completing the picture, there's a ground-hugging rosette of deeply dissected leaves, quite different from other meconopsis. *M. aculeata* is monocarpic and deciduous, vanishing entirely in winter and late to reappear. I thought I'd lost it and then suddenly, in mid-April, there it was.

There are some fifty Asiatic species of meconopsis, and one European woodland wildling, *Meconopsis cambrica*, the Welsh Poppy. It is reliably (indeed relentlessly) perennial in temperate gardens, with yellow or orange flowers and some named cultivars in redder shades or double-flowered. Though fetching in flower,

M. aculeata, the prickly poppy of Kashmir.

it's miserably scruffy thereafter. It's the only meconopsis I take pains *not* to grow. Once established in gardens, it's very difficult to get rid of, resurrecting itself freely from seed or bits of root. In short, a weed.

The Welsh Poppy is nevertheless the granddaddy of the genus. In 1814 it was the first to be given the name *Meconopsis* ("poppy-like") by the French physician and botanist Alexandre Viguier, who determined that it was not a true poppy as previously believed. From the start, however, there's been suspension of disbelief among scientists in accepting that a single, sea-level, European poppy should have an affinity with a tribe of plants resident a continent away and two miles closer to heaven. Now, through DNA analysis, there's some evidence they should be classified separately. The problem is that, by tradition, the botanical name always belongs to the first named—the type species: in this case *M. cambrica*. It follows that the Welsh Poppy would all alone remain a meconopsis, while some fifty Asiatic poppy species would have to be reclassified. A case of the tail wagging the dog.

Some brief encounters:

- I tried *Meconopsis robusta*, a skimpy version of the Satin Poppy with small yellow flowers. It's easy to grow, but not worth a place in the garden.

- *M. × harleyana*, the Ivory Poppy, is a lovely, natural hybrid between *M. simplicifolia* and *M. pseudointegrifolia*. I had a few seeds and managed to germinate just two, which died within weeks. If I ever get seed again, I'll give it another try.

- Struck out with *M. lancifolia*, a gorgeous, deep-purple poppy in the best forms, with the familiar habit of the smaller species—basal rosette, bare stem, single flower. I managed to bring a single plant to maturity, over-wintered and poised to bloom. Or, as it sadly turned out, poised to curl up and die.

- Better luck with *M. × beamishii* (*M. integrifolia* × *M. grandis*). No trouble in raising this usually monocarpic, cream-coloured poppy, named for the

The Welsh Poppy—the only meconopsis I take pains *not* to grow.

proprietor of the hotel in County Cork, Ireland, where it first appeared in 1906. But I found it ungainly, with untidy flowers more skim milk than cream, and therefore I did not save the seed. There are better versions, I know, and if seed from a different source comes my way, I'll give it another try.

- The "oak-leaved meconopsis," *M. villosa,* is a yellow-flowered woodland plant, growing at lower Himalayan elevations. Sturdily perennial and easily grown, it was first named *Cathcartia villosa* and has recently been booted back to that classification. Strike one pretty poppy from the meconopsis inventory.

A clashing chord? Maybe. But I like the dissonance of this hybrid primula with *M.* 'Hensol Violet' and *M.* 'Lingholm'. *Primula pulverulenta* provides background accompaniment in red.

M. 'Lingholm', honoured to be
the City of Edinburgh's official
floral emblem.

CHAPTER TEN

BLUE POPPY HEAVEN

... that featureless average of weather
which we know so well ...

FRANK KINGDON-WARD[1]

IN JANUARY 2004, THE CITY of Edinburgh adopted the Blue Poppy (*Meconopsis* 'Lingholm') as its official floral emblem, passing over a humble Scottish native, the purple sticky catchfly, also known as *Lychnis viscaria* or "Sticky Nellie."

Many wondered why the lowland capital of the land of thistle, furze and heather would make an honorary citizen of a native of remote mountains, which presumably none of the members of city council had ever visited. Sticky Nellie, councillors were reminded, was good enough to represent the city in a bouquet of flowers given to the Queen in her Jubilee year. The purple catchfly appeared to have the backing of the regular folk. Me too. Enamoured as I am of the Blue Poppy, my vote would have gone to Sticky Nellie. But in the lively, closely argued debate, pitting modesty against flamboyance, which culminated in this radical decision, council opinion was tipped by a submission from the Royal Botanic Garden, Edinburgh (RBGE). Their experts presented proof that the Blue Poppy in cultivation has a century-long association with that institution. They pointed out that a notable Edinburgh native, Sir George Taylor, botanist and one-time director of Kew Gardens, had in 1934 published the first comprehensive book on the Asiatic poppies and—the clincher—they showed that the Blue Poppy is very well adapted to the Scottish climate and easily grown in the city. So of course is Sticky Nellie, though perhaps better suited to the weed patch.

The Blue Poppy was pleased with this recognition and showed its appreciation at the Chelsea Flower Show in the spring of 2006, carrying off a bronze medal as the centrepiece in a simulated Sino-Himalayan landscape, designed and built by the City of Edinburgh parks staff at a cost of £30,000. The churlish murmured over this spendthrift use of time and money, saying that it were better spent on much-needed upkeep and improvement of parks and gardens within the city.

Indeed the Blue Poppy *does* grow very well in Scotland, the land of post-nasal drip, which is some compensation for the wretched, rheumatic weather. They flourish there like no place on Earth (including their alpine homeland), apart from equally suitable bits of cool Scandinavia.

The reason can be read in the weather. Lhasa, the capital of Tibet, has warm, wet summers with monsoon rain two days out of three and, on average, just two hours of sunshine a day. Heaven for poppies. Hellish humid for people. Edinburgh, the capital of Scotland, suffers cool, damp summers, average high 18°C, with somewhat drier winters. There are five hours a day of sunshine in July and four in August. Summers are wetter than winters. The Blue Poppy thrives on such misery.

In the Pacific Northwest where I grow meconopsis, Vancouver enjoys warm, dry, Mediterranean summers, with monsoon winters—one storm after another shouldering in from the Pacific Ocean. There are nine hours of sunshine a day in July and eight in August. Good for people, not so good for poppies.

Of course, the long-term averages for the Tibetan capital are not exactly applicable to the entire Himalayan range of the Blue Poppy. Nor is Edinburgh's weather exactly descriptive of southern Scotland, nor Vancouver's of the entire North Pacific coast. But the general shape of the rainfall graphs does apply throughout these regions.

In the Himalayas—wet summers, dry winters. In the Pacific Northwest, the opposite—dry summers, wet winters. Flip the convex curve of Himalayan rainfall, and it will roughly follow the concave curve of the Pacific Northwest

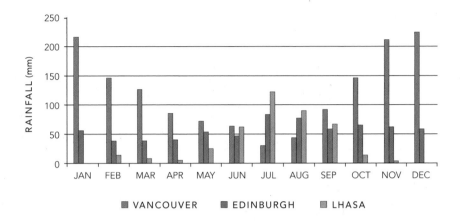

RAINFALL (mm)

250

200

150

100

50

0

JAN FEB MAR APR MAY JUN JUL AUG SEP OCT NOV DEC

■ VANCOUVER   ■ EDINBURGH   ■ LHASA

coast. Scotland offers a compromise, with Edinburgh conforming more to Lhasa than to Vancouver.

The Blue Poppies evolved in the Himalayas, genetically accustomed to the weather there, shrouded in drizzle as they leaf out and come into flower, the reverse of the Pacific Northwest in summer. But the Edinburgh region, where summer is a fleeting thing, occasionally omitted altogether, offers the poppies a growing season somewhat reminiscent of home.

I am tempted to move to Scotland.

※ ※ ※

While stopping short of making such a radical relocation, Rosemary and I did decide it was time to meet the Poppy People and see their meconopsis-rich gardens in flowering season, even though that would mean missing much of prime poppy time in our own garden. We decided on the first week of June. By then, on average, our Asiatic poppies would be on the wane and the Scottish collections, about two weeks later, in full bloom. But nature is not bound by averages and, as it turned out, this was not an average year. In both parts of the world, spring came late and flowering was delayed.

On arrival in Edinburgh, we were greeted by Evelyn and Lewis Stevens, who, like most first-rate gardeners, are grandparents, closer to the grave than the cradle. Lewis is energetic and outgoing, a robust man who had recently walked across Scotland. He likes to take advantage of the free rail pass provided to seniors in Scotland, boarding with his folding bicycle for exploratory excursions in the neighbouring counties. Evelyn prefers, on the whole, to limit her travels to the four corners of her garden. "The Blue Poppy has taken over my life," she admitted. Nevertheless, she generously found three days in her life to give to two Canadian visitors, taking us to meet some of the Poppy People and to see some of the most interesting plant collections in the adjacent counties.

Evelyn's delight in her big Blue Poppies was manifested in a pair of sparkling eyes as she spoke of her collection. In the rarefied international community of Blue Poppy fanciers, she is recognized as a world expert. Yet she was disarmingly unassuming about her achievements, not mentioning that in 2003 she was presented with an award for her distinguished contribution to Scottish horticulture. Nor did she make much of the fact that she's the holder of the National Plant Collection of "*Meconopsis* (large perennial species and hybrids)"—in short, the perennial Blue Poppy in all its forms.

The Stevens live in the country near Dunblane, a forty-minute drive from the Edinburgh airport. Their home is tucked in a protected hollow, a sanctuary of shelter amid acres of windswept, rolling sheep pasture. The abandoned wreckage of an old stone farmhouse occupied the centre of the three-and-a-half-acre site when they bought it. A perimeter of sycamore trees gave minimal protection from the prevailing winds. And that was it. Pictures from the 1980s illustrate a bleak landscape surrounding bits of wall and crumbling chimneys that stood there like rotting teeth. Sheep were grazing amid the rubble.

It must have required a free flight of the imagination for the Stevens to see what might be made of this desolate place. To begin with, they laid the foundations of the mature, mainly deciduous woods that now buffer Evelyn's garden on all sides, with naturalized drifts of daffodils and bluebells splashing the forest floor yellow and blue as the canopy leafs out in spring. Trees are Lewis's department, and he took the lead in the judicious selection and placing of a plantsman's collection of native and exotic species. He maintains them, too—a man's job, as tradition holds, in the best-regulated families. Lewis tends the trees, cuts the grass, grows the vegetables and takes on the heavy digging and delving. Evelyn grows the flowers.

In the mid-1980s, some of the original slate-roofed outbuildings were restored and a new house of stone built on the foundations of the old. The old farmhouse ruins were dismantled and the sandstone used to build patios and high garden walls, at which time their builder, Jimmy Bayne, entered their lives and set Evelyn off on a course she has pursued ever since—the quest for the perfect Blue Poppy.

An experienced grower of alpines and a long-time, prize-winning member of the Scottish Rock Garden Club, Evelyn had brought a patch of Blue Poppies to flower from a packet of commercial seed. Jimmy Bayne noted this and boasted, "Oh, I've got something much better than that." Some months later, he presented Evelyn with a clump of a perennial Blue Poppy from his own garden, a plant he'd rescued from imminent extinction on a building site some twenty

years before and the plant that would later officially be named *Meconopsis* 'Jimmy Bayne'.

Evelyn could tell at once that this was different from any Blue Poppy she had seen. Meconopsis are a hairy lot, but here she noticed a distinctive, reddish tone to the fuzz, specially at the conjunction of the stalk and its cluster of buds. The flowers were large and cup-shaped, somewhat purple when first open, with four well-rounded, overlapping petals. She and her plant enrolled in a meconopsis workshop at RBGE, where experts were unable to give it a name. She soon realized that this was just one of several unclassified and unnamed, infertile hybrids of this promiscuous genus. Finding, sorting, classifying and documenting these exceptional Blue Poppies has been at the centre of her life's work ever since. Being infertile, they can only be propagated by division. So what's the history of Jimmy Bayne's poppy? How did it come to be in the abandoned garden where he found it? Can its ancestry be deduced? What properties does it share with other infertile clones? How does it differ?

By tackling these questions and finding at least some of the answers, Evelyn can eventually determine whether a particular hybrid is, as 'Jimmy Bayne' proved to be, unique, or too similar to another to tell them apart. And if it is unique, is it *name-worthy*?

And if it is name-worthy, what then shall it be called?

There's more to Evelyn's garden than Blue Poppies. She's a collector of snowdrops and a connoisseur of trilliums. One of her snowdrops carries a bittersweet history. In March 1996, a rejected and deranged pedophile shot his way through a kindergarten class in Dunblane, killing the teacher and sixteen children, wounding all but one of the remainder before he turned one of his four guns on himself. Everyone in the small town was devastated by this unspeakable crime, including Evelyn, whose friend lost a five-year-old daughter. Evelyn named a snowdrop for the child, Sophie North. She dug up a fat bulb for me and now *Galanthus plicatus* 'Sophie North' is established in British Columbia.

With envy, I admired the ease with which she grows several varieties of celmisia, the New Zealand daisies with their silvery, silky leaves. Clearly, they flourish in her garden's cool, moist climate seven hundred feet (210 metres) above sea level, but these daisies are maddeningly impossible where I live. I coveted her scarlet candelabra primula, *Primula* 'Inverewe', an infertile, fragile beauty, named for the famous National Trust garden far to the north where it first appeared. I admired her high sandstone walls, with their hanging gardens of lewisias stuffed in holes, and mats of pink sandwort rooted in crevices. I particularly coveted the cheerfully spreading clumps of the two miniature poppies I have the devil of a time establishing at home—Farrer's Harebell Poppy, *M. quintuplinervia*, and the hybrid *Meconopsis × cookei*—though at least I don't have to contend with the rabbits (or maybe pheasants), which had beheaded many of the pink and lilac flowers. I was pleased to meet the shrubby, Scottish woolly willow, *Salix lanata*, with grey leaves soft as lambs' ears and fat, furry catkins sizzling with bumblebees. Being native and very much at home, it tends to stick its elbows out and must be rigorously pruned to prevent it from smothering other treasures. I stood in awe at the foot of a Korean fir, *Abies koreana*, which, fittingly, has *blue* cones.

"You really should have come *next* week," said Evelyn, repeatedly apologizing as if it were her fault that spring was late that year. This, of course, is what gardeners always say. That or: "You really should have been here *last* week."

To tour Evelyn's garden required close attention as she detailed the provenance of the big Blue Poppies, in prime time a parade of heartrending beauty, which, in part, we had to imagine because blooming time was late. Many had started to flower—clumps of *M. grandis*, always first off the mark, were almost over—and most had buds revealing a tantalizing wedge of blue, like a glimpse of thigh through a slit skirt. We met Cicely Crewdson's famous hybrid, brawny 'Willie Duncan', red-haired 'Jimmy Bayne' and Wedgwood-blue 'Bobby Masterton' with oddly shaped buds like stubby cigars. All these are among the very best of Blue Poppies and they're all infertile hybrids.

Evelyn pointed out 'Branklyn' (named for the famous public garden not far away, that holds a Blue Poppy Day each spring), and variations on this theme that

M. × cookei, 'Old Rose'.
A cheerfully spreading clump,
with *Primula* 'Inverewe'.

she was observing to see if they are sufficiently different to warrant separate classification. These Blue Poppy cultivars do not exist in the wild and most have occurred at random in various gardens. The distinguished exception is *M.* 'Slieve Donard', named for the century-old Northern Ireland nursery that acquired it from an Edinburgh gardener and put it on the market about fifty years ago—a hybrid, deliberately created in the mid-1930s. As we strolled among the poppies, Evelyn drew attention to the fine distinctions: the brilliant blue of 'Lingholm' and 'Slieve Donard', the darker, greyer hue of 'Sheldonii', 'Crarae', 'Dorothy Renton', 'Bryan Conway'—the show went on. She pointed out some provisionally nicknamed poppies: 'Clocktower', distinctive for being late-flowering, and 'Mophead', distinctive for the early unfolding of its huge, deep-blue flowers. We met dainty 'Dagfinn', named by Finn Haugli, retired director of the Botanical Gardens at Tromso, Norway, and a well-known meconopsis enthusiast.

I asked Evelyn if she had Betty Sheriff's "Dream Poppy," whose provenance is a real-life restaging of Novalis's fictional vision of the Blue Flower. After the war, George Sherriff, the plant collector, and his wife, Betty, liked to spend spring at a home they owned in the Sikkim hill station of Kalimpong. There, in the foothills of the Himalayas, they enjoyed a plant-hunter's paradise and magnificent views of Mount Kangchenjunga. As the story goes, while on a plant-hunting expedition, Betty dreamed that her husband came into her tent and told her of a ravishing Blue Poppy and exactly where it was growing. In her dream, he told her to go and collect it. So vivid was this vision that Betty hired guides and set out to find it.

The guides must have thought this was a foolish quest, but she did find her dream poppy and picked flowers to show George. Later, according to some accounts, the Sherriffs arranged for plants to be shipped to Scotland, where they were installed in the Himalayan garden they created together at their home, Ascreavie. The original plants have probably long gone, but seed and offshoots were shared and distributed among friends and fellow meconopsis lovers. And since then, through the familiar combination of loss and undocumented hybridizing, Betty's dream poppy has vanished into the dream from which it arose, or become diluted beyond recognition.

Red-haired 'Jimmy Bayne'

Brawny 'Willie Duncan'

Silky 'Slieve Donard'

Cicely Crewdson's hybrid

Smoky 'Sheldonii'

Pale 'Mildred'

Wedgwood-blue 'Bobby Masterton'

Bi-coloured 'Keillour'

"I don't believe it exists," said Evelyn.

If it did, Evelyn would have it, either in her garden, where large clumps of named Blue Poppies share space with other flowers and shrubs, or behind the house in trial beds, where cultivars are planted in short parallel rows. She has around eighty Blue Poppy cultivars. She has the species, too, exhibiting some of the subtle variations of form that have evolved in the wild, depending on where they're found.

Did I mention she's given her life to the Blue Poppies? The citation attached to the medal she was awarded in 2003 gives some idea of the scope of her commitment:

> She prepares material, monitors trials and makes countless, detailed observations. She has amassed a valued database. Many hours have been spent in herbaria, tracing introductions and tracking the origins of cultivars and species.

Not to mention collecting and starting seeds, nurturing seedlings, digging, dividing, planting and replanting, leading The Meconopsis Group (which she co-founded in 1998). I asked Evelyn who will carry on this work when she is no longer able. "I don't know," she replied regretfully, turning to check some poppies in five-gallon pots, being groomed for an important show in Edinburgh.

RIGHT AND PAGES 144–145
A chameleon, 'Barney's Blue' opens
clothed in purple, then changes to blue.

CHAPTER ELEVEN

MORE POPPY PEOPLE

She vows
to see heaven
now, for she has planted meconopsis, the holy
blue poppy that is not a poppy, but
the image of the sky just at
dusk, satin cut
from the wholeness of day, …

ELIZABETH PHILIPS[1]

LESLIE DRUMMOND HAD PREPARED A challenge for Evelyn Stevens: he had collected three wind-felled Blue Poppy flowers from different cultivars and placed them in separate bud vases. No leaves. Just the flowers on short stems. Evelyn's task was to identify them. One she quickly set aside. "That's Bobby Masterton." The others she examined with tender, intense interest. With the precision of a gemologist confronting a tray of sapphires, she stroked the petals, felt their weight. She knew from the shape of the flowers and the colour that one was 'Lingholm' and the other 'Slieve Donard'. But the eye alone cannot tell them apart. "This one," said Evelyn, running her fingers softly along the dark-blue petals, "is 'Lingholm'. I'm sure of it. 'Lingholm' has a crystallinity, a thickness in the petals which is lacking in 'Slieve Donard'. 'Slieve Donard' is more refined, more silky than 'Lingholm'."

Her identification was correct. Rosemary touched the petals to see if she could divine the difference. Well, maybe …

Leslie and Avril Drummond's garden, separated from the sidewalk by a low stone wall, can be enjoyed by anyone out for a stroll along the main street of the village of Lunanhead, near Forfar in eastern Scotland. It's a perfectly delightful, small, rectangular garden, sloping gently up to the Edwardian cottage that stands at the top of the property. A small, highly eclectic garden, crammed with treasure, reflecting the Drummonds' interest in collecting alpine plants, notably gentians, primulas and Asiatic poppies. If their garden has a plan, it's not immediately apparent. Plants are shoehorned in wherever the conditions should suit and wherever a scrap of space can be found. Organized chaos. Tall poppies grow through shrubs; short ones grow under shrubs, sheltered from that day's marrow-chilling wind.

In the narrow space behind the house, Leslie works at propagating from seeds and cuttings. All seed is started in boxes open to the rain, which sometimes splashes seed from one box to another. "I'm a very careless gardener," said Leslie, an elderly northcountryman, whose tousled and carefree appearance seems to complement his garden.

Leslie Drummond's particular passion is hybridizing. In nature, meconopsis hybrids (the crossing of two species) are rare and in gardens, most of the numerous hybrids, named or not, are accidental. However, some gardeners are at work hybridizing with intent, the intent to marry two different, desirable species and to produce something equally worth keeping, ideally combining the best features of each parent.

Leslie has been innovative in this art, creating new hybrids or recreating ones that were once in cultivation but since lost. His greatest contribution to horticulture so far was made when he crossed Farrer's Harebell Poppy, *Meconopsis quintuplinervia*, which is perennial, with *M. punicea*, which is not, and produced the perennial *M.* × *cookei* 'Old Rose', a gem of a poppy described earlier. 'Old Rose' is now a registered and much-sought-after garden plant. But he didn't stop there. Next he back-crossed 'Old Rose' with *M. punicea* to create '¾ punicea' and crossed that again with the parent to derive '⅞ punicea'—a pretty poppy displaying the hot red hue of *punicea* and the shapely form of × *cookei*. This new hybrid set seed and was

The Satin Poppy can grow to eight feet (2.4 metres). After flowering, the whole plant dies.

M. betonicifolia var. *alba*, with the customary golden stamens.

perennial, but nevertheless died out. Undaunted, Leslie is trying again. He riffled through a ledger, the meticulous documentation of his efforts over the years. "My ambition is to produce a perennial *punicea*," he said. "Whether this is possible I do not know."

He showed us how this artificial insemination is done. First, choose a fresh flower on the mother plant and pinch out all the pollen-bearing stamens. Then pluck stamens from a flower of the selected co-parent and rub these over the mother flower's stigma, covering it with pollen. If fertilization occurs, some of the resulting seed should carry genes from each parent. One of his hybrids was in bloom, a cross between two very closely related species of Farrer's Lampshade Poppy—*M. integrifolia* and *M. pseudointegrifolia*. The result, not surprisingly, bore large, luminous, yellow flowers.

"Of course," said Leslie, "this is all rather hit and miss. Even if it takes and you get good seed, you're just as likely to get a copy of one or other of the parents as a cross." Right. Mendel's Law.

As we left I asked Leslie for advice on germinating *Meconopsis punicea*. "Start the seed and put it in the fridge till January," he suggested.

On the way home to Dunblane, we called at Ian Christie's nursery. Evelyn said that when Ian was a lad, learning the trade and making deliveries for his employer, he frequently called at Ascreavie, where George and Betty Sherriff had retired in the 1950s. Major Sherriff, as Ian still refers to him, encouraged the young man's interest in plants and in particular fired a passion for the Blue Poppies that burns to this day.

Ian is a charter member of The Meconopsis Group, an exhibitor and an authority on the genus. At the nursery he provides space for the group's continuing Blue Poppy plant trials, as well as back-up for Evelyn's National Collection. Especially with rare varieties, Evelyn insures against loss by seeing that at least one other capable grower has a clone.

That afternoon, the nursery was battered by wind, which cancelled the warmth of the thin sunshine. It felt more like March than June. The Blue Poppy plants were drawn up in ranks of large pots, confronting this assault. Evelyn frowned as she inspected them.

"They look cold, don't you think?" A surprisingly anthropomorphic remark from Evelyn, a scientist whose observations are, more often than not, measurable.

"Really?"

"Yes. Do you not see how the leaves look unnaturally rigid?"

Indeed they did—huddled stiffly to the stem, quite unlike the relaxed posture of similar-sized plants in the partial shelter of an adjacent shade tunnel. Some were broken by the wind. Some flowers had raggedy-edged, scorched petals, singed by late spring frosts.

Evelyn was in some despair, wondering if it was worth all the effort. Her unwavering devotion to the Blue Poppy appeared to be shaken.

That far north, morning had broken before 4:00. Blackbird had spoken before 5:00. That morning, a cuckoo led the polyphonic dawn chorus in the Stevens' woods. *Cuckoo. Cuckoo.*

Evelyn was out with camera and tripod before 6:00, photographing the emerging flowers. The unaccustomed stretch of sunny days had drained the sky of blue and poured it into the poppies. Her spirits were quite restored. "Come and look at the 'Cruickshank' here. Would you not agree it's the most beautifully composed plant?" I would agree. Held clear of the foliage on slender stems, the flowers posed like a troupe of ballerinas ready to execute a pirouette.

We were on the road by 9:00, heading for Invergowrie, a village just west of Dundee, and a morning date with Henry and Margaret Taylor. They live on the inside corner of an L-shaped street, giving them substantially more garden space than their neighbours, which they use exquisitely. The Taylors are both renowned experts in alpine plants, long-time members of the inner circle of the Scottish Rock Garden Club, carrying off many trophies. In his mid-seventies, Henry still leads plant-finding expeditions in the Himalayas. Their native tongue is botanical Latin.

M. 'Cruickshank'—ballerinas about to execute a pirouette.

Their garden is immaculate. Plant areas are separated by curving paths of grass so crisp and even that I wondered if they might have been trimmed with nail scissors. Not a weed to be found. Margaret and Henry's collection is organized according to the specific needs of each plant group: sun or shade, peat or scree, acid or alkaline. Tufted buns of alpine species are tucked in holes drilled in porous, volcanic tufa; treasured miniatures are wedged in rock-wall crevices. *Micro*-micro-climates have been created, such as the large boulder of tufa planted on the sunny side with heat-loving saxifrages, while shade lovers, such as ramonda and haberlea, shelter on the cool, shady face.

"We can't grow meconopsis," said Margaret. "It's too dry." To prove it, she pointed to the mature spreading tree that commands a corner of the garden. Turning, I was greatly astonished to see an arbutus, Canada's only broadleaf evergreen. *Arbutus menziesii* is endemic to dry, rocky, usually south-facing sites along the shores of the Pacific Ocean from BC to Baja California. It seeds itself merrily in our garden. It has, I would have thought, no business being so much at home in eastern Scotland.

Despite Margaret's disclaimer, the Taylors can and do grow meconopsis, just a few rarities in this garden of rarities. Three I had never yet seen. First, the Ivory Poppy, *Meconopsis × harleyana*, a cross between *M. simplicifolia* and *M. pseudointegrifolia*, a rarity recorded by Kingdon-Ward in June 1924, growing in the company of its parents, on the open moorland above the Tsangpo River. It was named for the proprietor of the Scottish garden in which it spontaneously appeared in 1926. Since then the Ivory Poppy has been in and out of cultivation. Today it is in, thanks in part to the Taylors, who are well known for recreating this and several other hybrids.

M. delavayi, difficult, desirable and my most spectacular and consistent failure, was in full bloom here, a tidy clump in the shade of the arbutus tree. Père Delavay discovered this petite poppy in 1884 in northwestern Yunnan, but George Forrest is

*M. betonicifolia pratensis—
vanishingly rare.*

credited with introducing it to cultivation; it first flowered at RBGE in 1913. Rare in the wild and close to extinction in gardens, this perennial is a most fetching miniature. Several delicate six-inch (fifteen-centimetre) stems grow from a basal rosette, each stem supporting a disproportionately large, deep-purple flower. Henry Taylor grew it from seed and acknowledges there can be heavy losses at all stages of growth.

Rarest of all was a big Blue Poppy, *M. betonicifolia pratensis*, a very fine and exceptionally tall form of the Himalayan Blue Poppy, with flowers darker than the standard species and, to my eye, a puff of smoke in the colour. The Taylors got it from Betty Sherriff about twenty years ago. According to Mrs. Sherriff, the seed was collected by Frank Kingdon-Ward in northern Burma in 1926. Evelyn explained that this plant does not now set fertile seed and accordingly can only be propagated by division. Moreover, it's short-lived.

"It's a great rarity," she said, "and I don't know anyone anywhere who has it, apart from the Taylors and Fred Hunt next door to them—and me. It flowers well, but of course the flowering stems then die and the problem is it often produces very few offsets. If it ever fails to produce offsets, that will be the end of it."

As we said goodbye, I asked Henry if he had any advice on germinating *M. punicea*. "Well, some years ago I tried an experiment," he replied. "I soaked half a batch of seed for two days in a solution of gibberellic acid, then sowed the seed and compared results. It turned out that the soaking lessened the need for a cold spell." Gibberellic acid is a very potent hormone that occurs naturally in plants and controls their development.

*   *   *

We were invited to lunch at the home of James and Calla Cobb, who live in the village of Kingsbarns, close to the east coast of the county of Fife. Evelyn guided us across the bridge spanning the Firth of Tay, through St. Andrews, home of Scotland's oldest university, founded in 1413, but much better known as the home of golf. We were amazed to pass not one golf course, but six. A seventh was nearing completion. To paraphrase Oscar Wilde: so much land devoted to the unspeakable in hot pursuit of the uneatable.

James and Calla share their late-eighteenth-century cottage with William, a springer spaniel who likes to lie about in doorways and other places where he can be tripped over. Of all the Poppy People, James Cobb is the best known on account of his book *Meconopsis* (1989), which was the first published attempt to de-mystify the Blue Poppy and put its cultivation within reach of ordinary gardeners. In the preface, James said that his first sight of the Blue Poppy was a plant "considered to be a major selling point" in the garden of the house his parents bought when he was a teenager. A gardener from childhood, James acknowledged, with engaging self-deprecation, that his passionate pursuit of the Asiatic poppies may have had something to do with "the words of an honoured academic in my student days who advised that success was more often certain in science if one chose to be a world authority on something obscure."

James has the large and capable hands of a constant gardener. He works hard in the three high-walled gardens that the Cobbs maintain in Kingsbarns. Two are across the street. In these, James and Calla tend heritage fruit trees, free-range chickens of unusual breeds and all manner of berries and vegetables, enough to sustain them year-round and quite likely feed half the village, as well.

In the third, a shady garden behind the cottage, various meconopsis were growing, though few Blue Poppies. "I'm giving up on Blue Poppies. As I've grown older I've realized you have to stick to cultivating things that grow well. So I've shipped my collection way up north to my daughter's garden in Caithness where they thrive." James attributes the problem to climate change: drier and warmer in summer, colder in winter, noticeably less favourable to the Blue Poppies than thirty years ago.

Among his collection of tall Satin Poppies there was a stand of *M. wallichii*, the leaves and flowering stem rimmed with shimmering golden hairs. A perfect clump of purple *M. delavayi* was in flower, while *M. punicea* appeared to grow like a weed. I mentioned we'd seen them growing wild in the alpine meadows of Sichuan.

"Did you see any white ones?" asked James. "My ambition is to grow one." I didn't know such a thing existed.

Over lunch, James discussed the cultivation of meconopsis. His opinions sometimes cut across the grain of popular trends, such as the fad for raising Blue

Poppies from seed collected in the wild. "People like to boast, 'Oh I grew this from seed collected in Tibet,' as if that was something *organic*, pure and special. But just because it's wild doesn't mean it's a desirable plant. In fact there's a lot of spindly rubbish out there. Trouble is botanists collect this stuff and share seed with people who can't wait to get it going in their gardens. My fear is we're going to get inferior 'Lingholm' from cross-pollination."

On seed germination, James scoffed at the belief that this is difficult. "With the possible exception of mustard and cress, I can think of no seed that is easier to germinate than meconopsis." To prove his point he showed pans of *M. delavayi* and *M. punicea* seedlings, abundantly started from fridge-stored, four-year-old seed. He said he's even been able to germinate ten-year-old seed, provided it's been kept in the fridge. I mentioned my string of failures with *M. delavayi*, all dying within a few weeks of germination. James explained that this poppy is prone to a fungal attack and the solution he found was a very diluted spray of a fungicide called Octave, applied three times a year. Unfortunately, Octave is banned now, but James had some and gave me a pinch, a white powder that I took home, feeling every inch a drug-smuggler.

I asked James how he can be so successful germinating *M. punicea*. "The trick is to prevent the seed going into deep, double dormancy," he explained. "What you have to do is start the seed in summer as soon as it's ripe. Start it in a pot and cover with a fine mesh and then a deep layer of grit. Leave it outside. In January, pour off the grit, remove the mesh and germination will start. You can't miss."

This interesting man wrote on the flyleaf of his book, "For Calla, the perfect gardener's companion." Having spent an afternoon with the Cobbs, I think this ambiguous dedication appears to be apt in both its possible meanings. For Calla is obviously the perfect companion and helpmeet and, in addition, the greatest fan of James, the perfect gardener.

M. delavayi, rare in the wild and, in cultivation, subject to fatal fungal attack at all stages of growth.

"Blue, darkly, deeply,
beautiful blue."

CHAPTER TWELVE

HEAVENLY BLUE

Blue, darkly, deeply,
beautiful blue.

ROBERT SOUTHEY[1]

IS THERE A MORE BEAUTIFUL bloom in the entire flower kingdom than the fabled Blue Poppy? Is there a more *bluetiful* bloom?

The Lampshade Poppy (*Meconopsis integrifolia*), with its huge, pure-yellow flowers attracts admiration but does not enchant. The towering Satin Poppy (*M. napaulensis* hybrids), which in the best conditions can grow to eight feet (2.4 metres) with showers of blooms, commands respect for the achievement of the gardener but does not enthral.

But the cool, elusive beauty of the Blue Poppy draws paeans of praise. It stops people in their tracks. It radiates the azure of the unclouded vault of heaven, the cobalt of a white kitten's eye. It astonishes the senses, feasting on pigment of the utmost intensity. I have experienced a similar *épaté* in catching a glimpse of a mountain bluebird, or the iridescent blue morpho butterfly fluttering drunkenly across the tropical forest floor. Surprise has something to do with it. We *do not expect* a poppy to be blue.

Size has something to do with it too. In temperate-climate gardens, there's no comparably large sky-blue flower. We have bluebells and squills, delphiniums and forget-me-nots, hyacinths and hydrangeas. All blue, all pretty, all with trusses made up of many small flowers. All unsurprisingly familiar.

It's love at first sight. Gardeners tend to remember the first time they saw the Blue Poppy. When and where. A small milestone in life, like a first kiss.

But be wary; like that first kiss, it can draw you into its embrace and then without warning reject your affections, shun your tender loving care, scorn your promise of eternal fealty. For the Blue Poppy can be fickle, as those eager buyers discovered when they bought those fifty-dollar seedlings back in the mid-1920s—those first garden plants grown from Frank Kingdon-Ward's 1924 seed collection in Tibet.

For those who believe in the seven colour energies associated with chakra energy centres, auras and spectral emanations, blue is a mentally relaxing colour.

Blue has a pacifying effect on the nervous system. Blue is ideal for sleep problems, and hyperactive children. Buy them blue pajamas and paint their bedrooms blue.

Yes, popular colour psychology is used in marketing commodities from paint to carpets. From the carpet-buyers' handbook:

A SURVEY

Google calls up some 38,000 websites when "Himalayan Blue Poppy" is searched. A quick survey of the first two hundred revealed the following adjectives attached to those key words.
Positive:

Beautiful, breathtaking, bright, cherished, coveted, dazzling, decorative, delightful, divine, elusive (several), ethereal, exciting, exotic, exquisite, extraordinary, famous, fantastic, fine, glorious, gorgeous, incredible, inspiring, legendary (thrice), lovely, magical, majestic, mystical, mythic, mythical, perfect, popular, prized, rare (numerous), ravishing, rich, silky, spectacular, stunning, vibrant, vivid.

Negative (e.g. boring, overrated):
None.
The ayes have it. •

Blue is the most popular colour because it symbolizes sky and heaven.

Blue decreases heart rate and has a calming effect.

Blue produces the opposite effect of red.

Blue, with its peaceful, calming effect, works well in bedrooms.

Blue symbolizes loyalty, although it can be depressing.

And, according to *The Complete Book of Colour*, by Suzy Chiazzari: "Those who prefer blue have a yearning for a harmonious, tension-free existence. They are conservative, sensitive to the needs of others, and cautious. They make for loyal and trustworthy friends."[2]

There is some truth in all this, beyond a reasonable doubt. Psychologists have conducted numerous, credible experiments comparing the effect of colour on human physiology (blood pressure, heart rate, brain waves, eating behaviour). Red excites the central nervous system, increasing heart rate and skin temperature. Blue induces the reverse effects, slowing heart rate, lowering body temperature. *Blue with cold.* Blue offers a refuge from fearful red: the colour of fire and blood, the colour of *rage*.

People are more productive in blue rooms. Hence, blue is often used to decorate offices.

Some studies suggest that blue increases the performance of athletes, that weightlifters are able to handle heavier weights in blue gyms. As far as I know, no studies have been undertaken to determine if Blue Poppies improve the productivity of gardeners.

Looking for a job? Fashion consultants recommend wearing blue to interviews because it symbolizes loyalty. Sporting a Blue Poppy in the lapel should clinch it.

Wanting to lose weight? Some weight-loss plans recommend eating food off a blue plate. Blue, associated with food, is decidedly unappetizing. Do not paint the kitchen blue.

Blue is considered a business colour because it reflects reliability, as well as calm, stability, harmony, trust, truth, confidence, conservatism, security, cleanliness, order, loyalty—all the qualities you're looking for in a bank. For this reason, some political parties and businesses will choose blue, deep blue, as the prevailing colour in their logos. With all this going for blue, the company that adopts the Blue Poppy as its emblem should rule the roost.

There must be an innate, unconscious response to blue: a reassuring, calming signal sent by the brain to the heart in response to the serenity of a sunny day and still waters. The retina receives the environmental information. It is picked up by the visual cortex. Synapses fire the data to parts of the brain that regulate muscles, the heart and other organs. The brain issues instructions. All this in a nanosecond. *Relax. It's blue. A Blue Poppy.*

Blue flowers, such as forget-me-nots and violets, symbolize fidelity. Blue is the colour of constancy, hence "true" blue. According to an old English custom, the bride wears blue ribbons in her wedding gown and a blue sapphire in her wedding ring. Tiny flowers of blue speedwell are part of the wedding bouquet. Blue is the colour of devotion and innocence. The Virgin Mary is depicted in a blue robe. In China, blue is associated with immortality. For Hindus, blue is the colour of Krishna. For Jews, blue symbolizes holiness. Blue is the colour of hope. Blue is cool.

Perennial big Blue Poppies have been growing in gardens for about seventy years, a period matching my own lifespan. I reckon I have a good ten years of gardening ahead and I shall need them to realize certain ambitions. I want to coax at least one imperial-purple *Meconopsis delavayi* into flower in my garden and then see it bulk up as a perennial clump. I hope to cultivate a display of massed *M. punicea* and another of *M. simplicifolia*. I expect to do missionary work in the cause of the authentic, true-blue *M. grandis*, raising the plants for stocking botanic gardens and specialist collections in the bottom left-hand corner of Canada. Having seen how Leslie Drummond does it, I'm going to try some hybridizing, by means of hand pollination.

What the next seventy years will do to the cultivation of the Blue Poppy has everything to do with the bleak prospect of climate change. Hotter, drier summers and warmer, wetter winters are not suited to the delicate sensibilities of these plants. Perhaps they—and those who love to grow them—will

MY LOVE IS LIKE A BLUE, BLUE ROSE ...

Generations of rose breeders have sought the El Dorado of a blue rose. Their efforts have brought forth blooms of sickly hues resembling dead skin. Indeed, since roses entirely lack blue pigment, this quest can never succeed. However—enter the genetic manipulators. Can a gene for "blueness" be spliced into a rose?

It can. The largest Japanese distillery, Suntory, bored, one presumes, with whisky-making, bought the Melbourne, Australia, bio-tech company Calgene and changed its name to Florigene. After years of research and the investment of three billion yen ($USD 2.73 million), the partnership is said to have developed a blue rose, which may soon be released to the grateful market. To make a very complicated process ridiculously simple, the gene of the enzyme that produces the blue pigment, delphinidin, has been extracted from the petunia and activated inside the rose.

Suntory said: "Technologically, we are absolutely successful in creating a blue rose because of the blue pigment in the flower. But for our rose to be recognized by everyone to be blue, maybe we are only half way there."[3] Translation: they have probably produced a mournful mauve, rather like the "moon" series of carnations launched by the partnership in 1995.

Say it with flowers, but hold your applause. •

be driven to the shores of the Arctic Ocean.

In the wild, the poppies have no place to go. Himalayan glaciers are believed to be retreating at the rate of 33 to 49 feet (10 to 15 metres) each year, threatening water shortages for hundreds of millions of people, according to the World Wildlife Fund. Meconopsis may be threatened, too, along with other alpine plants. It is unlikely they will climb higher.

In the meantime, each spring, I'm drowning in blue.

The season starts with *M. grandis,* bursting from the bud in early April. *M. betonicifolia* starts to bloom a month later, along with its variations, the lovely 'Hensol Violet', named for Hensol Castle in the Scottish Borders where Lady Henderson grew it, and the equally desirable white form, *M. betonicifolia* var. *alba.* I have a particularly attractive version of the latter, with a cream-coloured centre rather than the standard golden anthers. As far as I know, this arose spontaneously in our garden. It comes true from seed. Throughout

I hope to cultivate a display of massed *M. punicea.*

May there's *M.* 'Lingholm' by the score and—my special favourites—a clump each of five infertile cultivars: 'Jimmy Bayne', 'Mrs. Jebb', 'Slieve Donard', 'Crarae' and 'Barney's Blue'.

Very important in assessing a Blue Poppy is the quality of the blue. It should stop you in your tracks. It should be clear, free of mauve or purple tints. It should be bold, the very essence of blueness. The flower should be big, four to six inches (fifteen centimetres) across, the petals rounded and over-lapping. 'Crarae' has all that. It's the closest I have come to finding my blue heaven.

The heavenly blue of 'Crarae'.

EPILOGUE

"What ARE you?" they ask me, curiously.
"A plant collector!"
"Yes, but what do you DO?" in a tone of exasperation.
"Why, collect plants," I say brightly.

FRANK KINGDON-WARD[1]

FRANK KINGDON-WARD WAS, AS his biographer Charles Lyte calls him, "the last of the great plant hunters," the last in a long line of explorers and plant collectors stretching back to the mid-eighteenth century. He was among the great because of his uncanny ability to judge a plant's suitability for British gardens and because no other man spent so long in the field or undertook so many expeditions over so long a period: twenty-four from 1909 to 1957, nearly half a century of exploration. At seventy-two, he was considering another venture in southeast Asia, when a stroke cut short his wanderlust.

He was the last of the great plant hunters because, as with those who went before, his vocation called for qualities of courage and endurance that are no longer necessary. Pain and fever were always hovering in the wings, though Kingdon-Ward was spared the fate of his contemporary, Reginald Farrer, who died in the mountains of northern Burma—"probably of pneumonia, brought on by a combination of poor nutrition, altitude sickness, living in a wet tent, physical exhaustion and the untrained use of an inadequate medical kit," in the professional assessment of his great-nephew, Dr. John Farrer.[2]

Today, help is never far away. The plant collector is not at risk of dying on the job.

Kingdon-Ward rode Tibetan ponies. His baggage train, besides the porters, was made up of mules, donkeys, oxen and yaks. Like George Leigh Mallory, he wore homespuns and tweeds with patched knees and elbows. His tent weighed sixty pounds (twenty-seven kilograms).

Contemporary plant hunters ride jeeps. They wear synthetic fabrics bought at specialized outfitters and bearing registered trademarks. Their base camp is often a well-appointed hotel, and when camping is necessary, they erect tents, weighing under eleven pounds (five kilograms), that will keep those inside warm and dry during a howling blizzard.

Modern explorers carry global positioning devices that can pinpoint their location to within a few metres. They are likely to be in the field for weeks rather than months. They take digital photographs and post them on Google Earth.

The 1924 expedition to the Tsangpo Gorges in Tibet started in April and lasted almost a year. For much of the time, Kingdon-Ward and Lord Cawdor were travelling in uncharted wilderness, surveying and making maps for the Royal Geographical Society, as well as collecting herbarium material (leaves, flowers and stems that were pressed and dried in the field) and, in due season, seeds. They suffered food shortages, persistent toothache and stomach pains, insect bites, blood-sucking ticks and leeches, fevers, periods of depression, drenching rains and cruel cold. In October, Kingdon-Ward was digging with his hands in the snow to collect the seed of plants he had located earlier.

Botanically and horticulturally, the expedition was of outstanding importance. Herbarium specimens were preserved, and seed later collected of some fifty rhododendron species, forty primulas and ten poppies (meconopsis). Most important of all, among the seed shipped home to England was that of the Himalayan Blue Poppy, *Meconopsis betonicifolia,* the plant for which Frank Kingdon-Ward is most gratefully remembered. From that collection are descended many of the Blue Poppies in gardens today.

Blooming season for the Blue Poppy in the alpine meadows overlooking the Tsangpo River is late spring. That is where, two hundred miles (320 kilometres) east of Lhasa, the plant hunter came upon his "stream of Blue Poppies, dazzling as sapphires in the pale light."[3] Not too far away, on Sunday, June 8, 1924, the mountaineer George Leigh Mallory vanished in the clouds surrounding the summit of Mount Everest. I like to imagine that these two historic events happened on the very same day.

※ ※ ※

In May 1995, a Himalayan expedition was approaching Mount Everest. This was not a party of plant hunters but a mountaineering expedition bent on standing at the top of the world. Whether or not they saw the Blue Poppy is not recorded.

Among the party was a young Australian. His name was George Mallory. Climbing in the footsteps of his grandfather, George Leigh Mallory, he hauled himself all the way to the top, reaching the summit at dawn on Sunday, May 14. There, with his ice axe, he chopped a hole and buried a picture of his grandfather, who thus—at least in spirit—achieved *his* blue heaven.

ACKNOWLEDGEMENTS

ELIZABETH PHILIPS MOST KINDLY OFFERED the stanza on "the holy blue poppy," from her poem "Witness." She embraces its allure in a few short beats. I am grateful to Andrew Moore for permission to use his translation from the German of Novalis's dream of the Blue Flower, and to Jennifer Schultz Nelson for allowing me to use her account of the chemical basis of the blue in the Himalayan Poppy.

James and Calla Cobb, Leslie and Avril Drummond, and Henry and Margaret Taylor, the Poppy People in Scotland, were all most hospitable in welcoming Rosemary and me, and sharing their love and knowledge of meconopsis. We were also generously treated at Les Jardins de Métis by Alexander Reford, Patricia Gallant and Jean-Yves Roy. Debbie Black, John Farrer, Grant Kennedy, Roger Morier, Gail Singer, Gerald Taaffe and Theo Terry have all made helpful contributions to this project, and Rob Forbes created the chart on page 131. Thank you all.

Without Theresa Kishkan's unflagging encouragement and support, *Blue Heaven* would probably have been put away in the bottom drawer. Her help and advice were invaluable in navigating the unfamiliar world of Canadian publishing.

I have been very fortunate in the publisher's choice of Marlyn Horsdal as my editor. Her eye for detail in copy editing is quite remarkable, but, more important, with tactful insistence, she challenged me to recognize and root out excess indulgence and irrelevance. This book is a far better thing, thanks to Marlyn's contribution.

Rosemary has helped in so many ways—copy editing, coming up with just the right turn of phrase when I turned to her for advice. Best of all, she has tolerated my preoccupation, indeed obsession, with the Blue Poppy and this project for several years. Thank you, Rosemary.

Finally, Evelyn Stevens, co-founder of The Meconopsis Group and my *Meconopsis* mentor. For ten years she has shared her experience and expertise with me. She has given me seeds of impeccable pedigree and plants of the finest standard. Without her tireless support of this Canadian outpost of The Meconopsis Group, my Asiatic poppy collection would be a sorry sight, while many other enthusiasts in the Pacific Northwest would lack the opportunity to raise high-quality Blue Poppies. Moreover, this book would not exist. Thank you, Evelyn.

ENDNOTES

OPENING QUOTATION

1   Edwinna von Baeyer and Pleasance Crawford, ed. *Garden Voices: Two Centuries of Canadian Garden Writing* (Toronto: Random House of Canada, 1995), 240.

CHAPTER ONE: "THAT LOVELY POPPYWORT"

1   *Gardeners' Chronicle*, 1881. Qtd. in Richard Aitken. *Botanical Riches: Stories of Botanical Exploration* (Melbourne: Melbourne University Publishing, 2008).

2   George Leigh Mallory, in a letter to his wife, Ruth, dated July 1922.

3   Qtd. in Charles Lyte. *Frank Kingdon-Ward: The Last of the Great Plant Hunters* (London: John Murray, 1989). 82.

4   Ibid.

5   Ibid.

6   Ibid.

7   Ibid.

8   Frank Kingdon-Ward. *Plant Hunting on the Edge of the World* (London: Cadogan Books, 1930), 55–56.

9   Ibid.

10 Qtd. in Lyte, 72.

11 Ibid, 74.

CHAPTER TWO: THE MYTH

1   Martha Houghton in *Bulletin of the American Rock Garden Society*, 1934.

2   Novalis. *Heinrich von Ofterdingen*. Andrew Moore, trans. www.members.ozemail.com.au (last accessed by author May 2008).

3   Graham Stuart Thomas in *Horticulture*.

4   Lewis Carroll. *Alice Through the Looking Glass*. In *Oxford Dictionary of Quotations* 3rd edition (London: Oxford University Press, 1980), 135.

5   Russell Page. *The Education of a Gardener* (London: Random House, 1983), 253.

6   Eleanor Perényi. *Green Thoughts* (New York: Vintage, 1983), 37–38.

7   Vita Sackville-West. *In Your Garden Again* (London: Frances Lincoln Publishers, 2004), 110.

CHAPTER THREE: IN THE STEPS OF CHINESE WILSON

1   John Ruskin. *Modern Painters* Volume IV. In *Oxford Dictionary of Quotations* 3rd edition (London: Oxford University Press, 1980), 411.

2   E. H. M. Cox. *Plant Hunting in China* (London: Collins, 1945), 138.

3   Jim Yardley. "In China, Skittish Pandas, Then Exploding Cliffs." *New York Times*, Asia Pacific Section. May 17, 2008.

3   George Taylor. *An account of the genus Meconopsis* (London: Waterstone 1985), 4–5.

4   Christopher Grey-Wilson. "Verifying a new *Meconopsis*." *The Garden* (RHS journal) Vol. 127 (December 2002), 930.

5   Charles Howard-Bury. *Everest Reconnaissance: The First Expedition of 1921* (London: Hodder & Stoughton, 1922), 106.

CHAPTER FOUR: THE BLUE POPPY

1   Frank Kingdon-Ward, attributed. Qtd. in Richard Aitken. *Botanical Riches: Stories of Botanical Exploration* (Melbourne: Melbourne University Publishing, 2008).

2   George Taylor. *An account of the genus Meconopsis* (London: Waterstone, 1985), 69.

3   Frank Kingdon-Ward. *Plant Hunting on the Edge of the World* (London: Cadogan Books, 1930), 301.

4   Kenneth Cox, ed. *Frank Kingdon Ward's Riddle of the Tsangpo Gorges* (London: Garden Art Press, 2001), 125.

CHAPTER FIVE: DESPERATE MEASURES

1   Anne Scott-James. *Perfect Plant, Perfect Garden* (New York: Fireside, 1988), 125.

CHAPTER SIX: ELSIE'S EDEN

1   Letter to Frank Kingdon-Ward from Elsie Reford, c. 1930. Qtd. in Alexander Reford. *The Reford Gardens* (Quebec: Les Editions de l'homme, 2004), 142.

2   Frank Kingdon-Ward. *The Garden Beautiful*. Vol. 9, Num 4. (North Vancouver, July 1946), 15.

3   Kenneth Cox ed. *Frank Kingdon Ward's Riddle of the Tsangpo Gorges* (London: Garden Art Press, 2001), 101.

4   Ibid, 94.

5   Ibid.

6   Ibid, 116.

7   Ibid, 136.

8   Frank Kingdon-Ward, attributed.

CHAPTER SEVEN: GET GROWING

1   Qtd. in David Pratt. *The Impossible Takes Longer* (Vancouver: Douglas & McIntyre, 2007), 3.

2   Dr. Jennifer Schultz Nelson, Ph.D. University of Illinois Extension. web.extension.uiuc.edu (last accessed by the author May 2007).

CHAPTER EIGHT: KEEPING UP APPEARANCES

1   E. B. White, attributed.

CHAPTER NINE: THE RAINBOW COLLECTION

1   James L. S. Cobb. *Meconopsis* (Portland: Timber Press, 1989), xi.

2   Samuel Beckett. *Worstward Ho.* Qtd. in David Pratt. *The Impossible Takes Longer* (Vancouver: Douglas & McIntyre, 2007), 3.

3   Reginald Farrer. *The Rainbow Bridge* (London: Cadogan Books, 1986), 229.

4   Kenneth Cox, ed. *Frank Kingdon Ward's Riddle of the Tsangpo Gorges* (London: Garden Art Press, 2001), 104.

5   Ibid.

CHAPTER TEN: BLUE POPPY HEAVEN

1   Qtd. in Charles Lyte. *Frank Kingdon-Ward: The Last of the Great Plant Hunters* (London: John Murray, 1989), 82.

CHAPTER ELEVEN: THE POPPY PEOPLE

1   Elizabeth Philips. *A Blue with Blood in it.* (Regina: Coteau Books, 2000), 31.

CHAPTER TWELVE: HEAVENLY BLUE

1   Robert Southey. *Madoc* (1805). In *Oxford Dictionary of Quotations* 3rd edition (London: Oxford University Press, 1980), 514.

2   Suzy Chiazzari. *The Complete Book of Colour* (Boston: Element Books, 1988).

3   www.florigene.com (last accessed by the author May 2007).

EPILOGUE

1   Michael Pollan, ed. *In the Land of the Blue Poppies: The Collected Plant-Hunting Writings of Frank Kingdon-Ward* (New York: Modern Library, 2003), 4.

2   John Farrer in conversation with the author. April 2008.

3   Frank Kingdon-Ward, attributed. Qtd in Richard Aitken. *Botanical Riches: Stories of Botanical Exploration* (Melbourne: Melbourne University Publishing 2008).

SELECT BIBLIOGRAPHY

Cobb, James L. S. *Meconopsis*. Portland: Timber Press, 1989.

Cox, E. H. M. *Plant Hunting in China*. London: Collins, 1945.

Cox, Kenneth, ed. *Frank Kingdon Ward's Riddle of the Tsangpo Gorges*.
   London: Garden Art Press, 2001.

Grey-Wilson, Christopher. *Poppies: the Poppy Family in the Wild and in Cultivation*.
   London: B.T. Batsford, 1993.

Jermyn, Jim. *The Himalayan Garden: Growing Plants from the Roof of the World*.
   Portland: Timber Press, 2001.

Kincaid, Jamaica. *Among Flowers: A Walk in the Himalaya*. Washington, DC: National Geographic
   Directions, 2005.

Kingdon-Ward, Frank. *Plant Hunting on the Edge of the World*. London: Cadogan Books, 1985.

Lyte, Charles. *Frank Kingdon-Ward: the Last of the Great Plant Hunters*. London: John Murray, 1989.

Pollan, Michael, ed. *In the Land of the Blue Poppies: The Collected Plant-Hunting Writings of Frank
   Kingdon-Ward*. New York: Modern Library, 2003.

Reford, Alexander. *The Reford Gardens: Elsie's Paradise*. Quebec: Les Editions de l'homme,
   2004.

Taylor, George. *An account of the genus Meconopsis*. London: Waterstone, 1985.

Stevens, Evelyn and Christopher Brickell. "Problems with the Big Perennial Blue Poppies"
   Scottish Rock Garden Club Journal, #107, 2001.

Terry, Bill and Evelyn Stevens. "Seed Trials of Meconopsis 'Lingholm'"
    Scottish Rock Garden Club Journal, #116, 2006.

The Meconopsis Group website. www.meconopsis.org

INDEX